Opinions Matter

"The book attempts a comprehensive review of the problems and prospects of MSME sector in India and presents an objective analysis of its strengths and weaknesses. Given the immense potential for employment generation, the sector needs to be nursed carefully, particularly in the face of global challenges of competitiveness and market volatility. The author painstakingly takes us through the virtual minefield that an entrepreneur has to survive to stay afloat. Especially insightful are his observations on the role the Financial Institutions (FIs) have to play in this process. All in all, a notable addition to the literature on the subject."

–**B.P. Acharya**, IAS
Special Chief Secretary, Government of Telangana

"The book has comprehensively covered the need of the sector and the unrealised potentials it offers. The never-ending issues of capital and adequate working capital from the lending institutes have been a perennial roadblock for the sector. Though the scenario has favourably changed over time, the sector still merits more attention and care. Though there have been plethora of directives both from the RBI and GoI, case studies amply prove that the lack of timely flow of adequate credit exists.

The author's mastery over the subject is a product of his formidable engagement with the policy and its implementation. This book would very well serve those who are in policy formulation, research and academics."

–**Amitabha Guha**
Former Deputy Managing Director, State Bank of India

THE STORY OF INDIAN MSMEs

Despair to Dawn of Hope

B. YERRAM RAJU

Foreword: Duvvuri Subbarao, Former RBI Governor

KONARK

Konark Publishers Pvt Ltd
New Delhi • Seattle

Konark Publishers Pvt. Ltd
206, First Floor,
Peacock Lane, Shahpur Jat,
New Delhi 110 049
Phone: +91-11-41055065
e-mail: india@konarkpublishers.com
website: www.konarkpublishers.com

Konark Publishers International
8615, 13th Ave SW,
Seattle WA 98106
Phone: (415) 409-9988
e-mail: us@konarkpublishers.com

Cataloging in Publication Data--DK
Courtesy: D.K. Agencies (P) Ltd. <docinfo@dkagencies.com>

Raju, B. Yerram, 1941- author.
The story of Indian MSMEs : despair to dawn of hope / B. Yerram Raju ; foreword: Duvvuri Subbarao.
pages cm
Includes bibliographical references and index.
ISBN 9788193555491 (HB)
ISBN 9788194201809 (PB)

1. Small business--India. 2. Manufacturing industries--India. 3. Economic development--India. I. Title.

LCC HD2346.I4R35 2019 | DDC 338.6420954 23

Edited by Deepak Goel
Cover Jacket by Dushyant Parasher
Typeset by Saanvi Graphics, Noida
Printed and bound at Thomson Press (India) Ltd.

This book is dedicated to my mentor T.L. Sankar, a civil servant; recipient of the third-highest civilian award of the country, Padma Bhushan; and one who in his lifetime served the cause of small enterprises with empathy and devotion. His inspiration is my elixir.

T.L. Sankar is also the architect of energy reforms. He spent all his leisure for the cause of the small enterprise sector.

He decorated every post he held, namely Director, Institute of Public Enterprise; Director General, NIRD, Hyderabad; and Principal, Administrative Staff College of India, Hyderabad.

It is difficult to imagine that he is not amidst us. He died on 26 December 2018.

Contents

EMPLOYMENT
INNOVATION
MSME
?
BPK.

Foreword

Economic development poses many complex challenges. Promotion of micro, small and medium enterprises (MSMEs) figures somewhere on top of that list. Everyone agrees on the virtues of the MSME sector—they are an integral part of the value chain, are job intensive and contribute more than proportionately to exports. Also importantly, because they can be geographically dispersed, they aid development of regional economies and restrain urban migration. Yet no developing country has been able to fully exploit the promise of the MSME sector. India is no exception.

There has been no shortage of innovative policies; on the contrary, there has been a surfeit of them. Over the last seven decades since Independence, both the Centre and states across the country have unveiled a variety of policies and initiatives to promote the MSME sector. The main bottleneck has been in their operationalisation.

The problems that have daunted the MSME sector are a familiar litany: shortage of capital, red tape, bureaucracy, corruption and most of all lack of sympathy and understanding at the operational level. Notwithstanding pious intentions and bold promises, there is no one to handhold a small entrepreneur in distress. Nor is there a feedback loop from lessons of experience to policy.

It is here that this book by Dr B. Yerram Raju, *The Story of Indian MSMEs: Despair to Dawn of Hope,* adds tremendous value. He brings to the book decades of 'frontier' experience in his diverse roles as banker, consultant and mentor. Furthermore, over the last few years, he has been an advisor to the Telangana Industrial Health Clinic Limited (TIHCL) with the mandate of handholding MSMEs in distress and reviving them to health through comprehensive advice, guidance and mentoring. The work that he has done with TIHCL has further added to his understanding of the operational level challenges of MSMEs.

This book reflects that rich experience and expertise. What adds further value to the book are the case studies which give us an understanding of the complex challenges that entrepreneurs confront and the dilemmas that bankers face. Drawing from these lessons of experience, Dr Raju makes very instructive policy recommendations covering the entire life cycle of an MSME—starting, running and closing.

Written with his trademark passion and commitment, this book will be especially useful for policymakers at the operational level, finance sector professionals, economic analysts, researchers, students, and most of all current and aspiring entrepreneurs.

20 March 2019 **Duvvuri Subbarao**,
Former RBI Governor

Preface

When there is plenty of literature on the subject of micro, small, and medium enterprises (MSMEs), with a flurry of articles in popular financial media and several research outputs that include periodical releases from the World Bank, McKinsey, Boston Consulting, KPMG, Industry Associations etc., where is the need for another book? The need arose due to the complexity of the sector, performance shortfall—sometimes driven by policy prescriptions—inadequate enterprise development initiatives, and renewed emphasis on the sector led by global markets. While several of them laid emphasis on the missing 'middle' in MSME sector, I feel it is this 'medium-the middle' that took advantage of most of the schemes while the cradles of innovation in manufacturing, micro and small escaped attention of stakeholders and the policies invariably encouraged their horizontal expansion instead of vertical expansion.

This book proposes to lay more emphasis on the manufacturing MSEs' access to finance and its drivers. Government of India (GoI) has taken a slew of initiatives during 2015-18 to strengthen the sector. It has pleaded with the Reserve Bank of India (RBI) to take appropriate measures to ensure easy and timely access to credit. An interesting aspect of this book is the references to the author's own articles published in various financial and other dailies, journals, and blogs. The pan-India case studies add strength to the perceptions.

Murthy, hailing from Srikakulam in Andhra Pradesh, completed his engineering from Andhra University in the 1970s, and picked up some experience in a few reputed mechanical engineering firms. On seeing an advertisement in a daily, that qualified engineers thinking of setting up small-scale industries as ancillaries to Hindustan Aeronautics Limited (HAL) and Bharat Heavy Electricals Limited (BHEL) would get space in Jeedimetla Industrial Estate, he decided to try his luck. He started the unit with a small capital, and SBI gave the working capital based on the order of HAL. He experienced the bureaucratic delays in securing permits for running the factory; getting power supply to the unit; satisfying the labour inspectors who would visit the factory periodically, etc. In a way, he had the full experience of inspector raj—with a minimum of 100 inspections, and submission of as many as 60 returns to various departments, including environmental and pollution clearances. Though he did not have a furnace of boiler, he still had to submit those returns, he rues. After three and a half decades, during which he also worked as president of the Industry Association and the Federation of Associations, he exited after liberalisation under pressure of his children.

Gopal, an electrical engineer, had set up an ancillary unit to BHEL to supply components. After two decades of experience as an entrepreneur, he decided the knowledge of law is crucial to run an enterprise, as he was paying a huge price for his honesty. He joined the Evening College of Law in Osmania University. After securing the degree, he practiced as a junior to a reputed advocate in the High Court. During this period, he continued to run the industry. After 25 years, he sold away the unit and settled as an advocate. His knowledge of the industry helped him argue the case of the industries before the Electricity Regulatory Authorities (ERA) after liberalisation on tariff fixation. Further, he won the reputation of being a professional of high competence. He is now a leading advocate in the Supreme Court.

One characteristic trait shared among all such qualified persons was the passion to run the enterprise, come what may. But except one, all others retreated, and bowed to the system. All of them unequivocally say laws and rules bow before those who interpret them according to their benefit. They concede it is a great challenge to run a small enterprise in India. Producing a quality product is one thing, but receiving the price for it is another. Contracts were invariably in favour of the large industry—public or private. Delays in payments had to be accepted. Large industry always got better attention from the banks for working capital limits and security. They also got better interest rates than them. The large industry similarly enjoyed their working capital by delaying the bills because they were all captive suppliers.

In fact, post-liberalisation, sincere efforts were initiated with the help of bureaucrats to mend the laws. This resulted in the single window system for approvals in Kerala and AP. Not convinced with such levels of progress, they felt there was a need for the industry to take over the infrastructure from the local authorities. On these lines, an effort was initiated by the then commissioner of industries and secretary to the state government to establish an Industrial Area Local Authority (IALA) in AP, with industrial estates as the focal points. These IALAs, on a shared revenue basis, collected complete local taxes and shared a certain proportion of it with the municipal corporations. They also maintained the infrastructure in the industrial estates. This gamut of operations led to the clean-up of the industrial corridors formerly part of AP.

All of them agree, the situation after liberalisation gradually improved in terms of law and facilitation. However, the mindset of the banks and the line staff in the industry still had a lot to change.

This book, *The Story of Indian MSMEs: Despair to Dawn of Hope*, is about the policy initiatives of both the Union and state governments, and the journey of a few small entrepreneurs viewing failure as a stepping stone to success. In the lifecycle of an enterprise, development and death co-exist at different times. The development process involves struggle; walking on rugged roads, and unwelcoming infrastructure in some cases.

I have published three books, and over 100 articles, on the sector from time to time. If this book serves as a wake-up call to some entrepreneurs, and a guide to the future of policy pursuits in this sector, it would achieve its purpose. The access to finance continues to draw the ire of entrepreneurs, and adequate attention to it can be found in this book.

Several state governments have innovated in the policy space. Some of these policies can be found in the annexure.

This book is also about how the sector has been progressing over the years, and asserts the future is not going to be a repetition of the past. Global interventions have been influencing the markets, systems, and the ways in which the enterprises function.

T.V. Gopalakrishnan, Retd. RBI Chief General Manager, M. Sanjaya, former RBI General Manager, and Subbaiah Singala, Faculty, College of Agricultural Banking, have been supportive of my views, and contributed to the ruminations on this subject. I am also thankful to the *Hindu BusinessLine*, *Moneylife*, and *KNN India* for publishing several of my articles that have been used in this book.

I must say my wife Satyavati and my daughters have always been indulgent to my academic pursuits of excellence. Their affection and sweet smiles are always a source of energy to me.

Paul Ryan, former speaker of the US House of Representatives, says: 'Behind every small enterprise, there is a story worth knowing.' I will add, there is a lesson worth learning. I am beholden to several enterprises whose cases in *nom de plume* have enriched my learning.

I am thankful to Jaggarao, former Chief Manager, Bank of India for taking the pain to go through my articles, and put them in order to shape it into a book; Ms Bhavani, executive, Telangana Industrial Health Clinic Limited (TIHCL) for helping me in formatting the document, and Ms Divya for updating the statistical tables where needed. Ms Lekshmi Parameswaran, editorial associate of Konark Publishers, New Delhi, deserves special thanks for raising a few key observations on the draft book that helped me refine the content significantly.

I am short of words to express my gratitude to Duvvuri Subbarao, former Governor, Reserve Bank of India for agreeing to script the Foreword amidst his busy schedule.

I am grateful to B.P. Acharya, IAS, Special Chief Secretary, Government of Telangana, for his encouragement and the manifestation of the essence of the book in the cartoon.

1

Introduction

Any discussion on MSMEs starts with 'they are the engines of growth' and 'they significantly contribute to employment and exports'. MSME sector contributes 25 per cent to the country's Gross Domestic Product (GDP), and 32 per cent to the Gross Value Added (GVA) (Economic Survey 2018, GoI), 45 per cent to the manufactured output (Ministry of Commerce and Industry) and 40 per cent to the exports. The labour to capital ratio in MSMEs, and the overall growth in the sector, is much higher than the large industries. The geographic distribution of the MSMEs is also more even.[1] Thus, the MSMEs are viewed popularly as effective instruments of inclusive growth. But, they are also viewed as risks to themselves and the institutions that contribute to their growth. Many of the risks associated with them are viewed as more self-perpetuating than external. Although, a critical look at them would help resolve many such perceived risks with circumspection and efficient externalities. This chapter proposes to discuss most of them, and look at the objective ways in which risk management could help overcome the prejudices ascribed to them.

Seedbeds of entrepreneurship

Dinesh Awasthi, former Director of the Entrepreneurship Development Institute of India (EDII) noted that 'Economic growth is effect, entrepreneur is the cause. Entrepreneurs explore opportunities, convert ideas into viable business proposition, and provide new products and services to the society by bringing together and combining various factors of production. They change life style of the people.'[1]

Industrial policies since Independence engaged the focused attention of the government, the inter se priorities changed with each Five-Year Plan. The Industries Development and Regulation Act (IDRA) of 1951 provided the basic framework for the post-Independence industrialisation strategy. Since the model for industrialisation in the 1950s was based on capital-intensive heavy industries, the priority of employment generation fuelled the development of widely dispersed, mass consumption-good producing, labour-intensive, small-scale industries. As the process of economic development led to changing priorities, the policy focus shifted to addressing regional imbalances (1977), facilitating linkages between large firms and their subcontractors (1980), and finally boosting exports, especially from rural areas (1990). However, the government controlled the entire industrial activity through the industrial licensing system; trade and foreign investments also had similar controls at the entry point. A whole host of subsidies, concessions, and government support were pumped in the economy through protective policies of the GoI in favour of the small industries.

Though deregulation is, nowadays, accepted as the basic thrust of industrial policy, the precise contours and the extent to which the process of deregulation can be carried out, its limits, and the type of interventions that must remain even in a deregulated system are issues which still remain open. The quasi-federal Indian system has had a major influence on the implementation of industrial policies with the Centre formulating policies and the states having a good deal of flexibility to pursue their own policies. Consequently, there are central laws, central laws with rules framed by the state governments, and state laws and rules.[2] The fact that regulations raise the cost of doing business shouldn't, however, be understood to mean that it should be done away with: environmental standards, for example, impose a cost on the business sector, but these costs may be outweighed by the social benefits of improved environmental quality.

For those who would like to know the origins of small-scale industries (SSI) and the MSMEs later, one should look at a wayside welder, carpenter, machine repairer, who had set up his shop with a small capital from the family silver, or his own savings. The large public sector undertakings (PSUs) promoted ancillary industries as vendors. These small industries were set up by the engineering and technology graduates, or diploma holders, or persons with native skills, with the support of the state incentives in capital investment, and the debt capital coming from the banks. They had all set up the industrial units with passion. They had confidence in their abilities to produce a product, or provide a service. No enterprise is set up with a view to sell away his/her property, but to gain a profit and lead a social life better than what his/her parents and grandparents led.

There are certain categories of small industries that cater to project services to the sectors like defence, aerospace, oil and natural gas, steel, fertiliser equipment. These project services start from designing stage to delivering the equipment or their components. Such types of industries have to accommodate the changes dictated by the principals, owing either to competitive pressures or external compulsions. There are other small industries that need to fall in line with the competitive environment and market forces, and graduate to a higher scale of production, quality at lower costs. These self-funded proprietary firms, private co-operatives, private self-help groups, Khadi, and village and coir industries, not only provide huge employment opportunities but also ensure regional balance by taking industrialisation to rural, remote and less-developed areas (about 20 per cent of the MSMEs).

There are, however, certain enterprises set up with an eye on public resources available that can be taken advantage of for private comfort for a short time. These would end up as wilful defaulters for certain. Subsequent to post-nationalisation of banks, priority sector categorisation provided easy access to the debt capital from the public sector banks (PSBs) in a designated proportion to the overall debt of the banks.

It will be intriguing to see how they are defined across the globe, and in India. In fact, the definition of MSME in India has become contentious.

Notes

1. Dinesh Awasthi, "EDII-ADFIAP-Cambodia presentation," Cambodia, 18 November 2010.
2. B. Yerram Raju, *Small Industries in India, Policies and Perspectives in the Emerging Context* (New Delhi: Gitam-Excel Publishers, 2004).

2

Definitions of MSMEs - Contentious

Global definitions of MSME

There is no common yardstick by which small and medium enterprises are defined. The definition varies from country to country, taking into account different quantitative (Raju, 2004: p. 4) and qualitative (Ibid: p. 11) variables. The most commonly used are: annual turnover, total assets, number of employees, average annual receipts or capital. Usually, no attention is given to the legal form, but independence from big enterprises, work organisation and industry type are often considered. In view of all these different criteria, the Basel Committee has mainly chosen to follow the annual turnover definition, setting the same general rules to calculate the capital requirements for all the firms (large, medium and small), but ensuring a lighter treatment for small and medium ones (with annual turnover less than €50 million).

For long, the small enterprise sector in India was equated only with small manufacturing enterprises, defined by investment in plant and machinery. With the formulation of the Micro Small and Medium Enterprise Development Act 2006, there was a paradigm shift recognizing services also as part of small enterprise promotion and development and enlarging the scope to medium enterprises after redefining the micro sector. The definition of MSMEs in India on this count admits only medium enterprises for consideration of Basel III risk dispensation.

Definition of Micro, Small and Medium Enterprises (Manufacturing and Service)

Sector	Manufacturing	Services
	{Enterprises* engaged in Manufacturing or production of goods pertaining to any industry specified in the first schedule to the Industries (Development and Regulation) Act 1951}	{Enterprises* engaged in providing or rendering services}
Micro Enterprises	Where the investment in Plant & Machinery does not exceed Rs 25 lakh	Where the investment in equipment** does not exceed Rs 10 lakh [**currently called as Small Scale Service/ Business Enterprises (SSSBEs)**]
Small Enterprises @	Where the investment in plant and machinery is more than Rs 25 lakh but does not exceed Rs 5 crore	Where the investment in equipment is more than Rs 10 lakh but does not exceed Rs 2 crore
Medium Enterprises	Where the investment in Plant & Machinery is more than Rs 5 crore but does not exceed Rs 10 crore	Where the investment in equipment is more than Rs 2 crore but does not exceed Rs 5 crore

These outdated definitions of MSMEs are set to change consistent with growth of the Indian economy. The Union Ministry of MSME introduced in Parliament in July 2018 an Amendment to the MSME Development Act 2006 to redefine the sector basing on annual turnover as the single criterion. However, the changes that occur should have focused attention on manufacturing sector that has taken a backseat since 2006.

As per the proposed amendment, any business with a turnover of up to Rs 5 crore would be considered as a 'micro enterprise'. A 'small enterprise' would be one whose annual turnover is more than Rs 5 crore but not exceeding Rs 75 crore. Those businesses with turnover over Rs 75 crore but up to only Rs 250 crore would be deemed as a 'medium enterprise'.

However, the Bill is still pending in Parliament for approval. While change in the definition from the sole criterion of investment in plant and machinery that has facilitated Inspection Raj is long overdue, again moving to single criterion of turnover is fraught with greater risks than before for the MSMEs.

Globally, MSMEs are the backbone of the economy with some definitions showing their contribution accounting for 95 per cent of the world's GDP.

The term 'SME' encompasses a broad spectrum of definitions. The definition varies from country to country. Generally, these guidelines are based upon either headcount or sales or assets or a combination of any two or all of them. Some are backed by law while others by practice and policy.

Definitions vary across the multilateral institutions like the World Bank, UNIDO, and OECD, etc. World Bank defined SMEs based on Employment and Assets. Out of 18 countries in Asia, the Caribbean, East Africa, West Africa, South Africa, Latin America, North America and Eastern Europe, six countries defined it in terms of Assets, Employment and Turnover. Nine countries defined in terms of two of the three criteria—either assets and employment or employment and turnover.

Only four countries, including India, defined SMEs in terms of a single criterion—assets or employment. The Philippines, Thailand, Bolivia, Mozambique and Rwanda defined it in terms of a single criterion, employment. This single criterion is also not perfect. Employment as a criterion to define the sector has widely been prevailing. Number of employees by itself is no indicator for efficiency of the enterprise. It is also no guarantee for growth. In fact, there would be a positive effect of economic growth on jobs. This criterion applied singly has again the consequence of services sector like the IT getting undue advantage as even 10 employees can contribute to a turnover of Rs 500 crore annually.

When the Indian economy is set to be the third largest in the world with increase in WB rankings of Ease of Doing Business, it is important to ensure that each segment of the economy, more so the sector that has the largest potential for employment creation and enterprise promotion, moves in tune with the developed economies.

Indian MSMEs that significantly contribute to economic growth are already suffering several disabilities and while resolving one, leading to many more would be disastrous. The objective of change in definition of the sector should be providing jobs, wealth and innovation.

Turnover as a single criterion has the deleterious consequences of over-flexibility. It also has the immediate consequence of picking up NPA status with the turnover threshold of Rs 75 crore annually for the small and Rs 500 crore for the medium. Presently, the gross NPAs of the MSME sector stand at around 7-8 percent.

Depending on trade cycles, the turnover may increase or decrease the redefined thresholds. Whenever such change occurs, it would be well-nigh impossible to reclassify and extend or withdraw the entitlements of incentives, wherever available for this sector. It will be preposterous to presume that GST would resolve the moving turnover thresholds for qualifying the enterprise in a particular category. Obtaining credit would become more difficult.

Any two criteria defining the sector would be more rational and lead to better growth of the sector. Doing away with investment in plant and machinery is welcome but replace them with employment and turnover. It will also be possible to attract more global investments into the sector. This would help MSMEs in engaging labour on more competitive terms than now and also measuring their contribution to the turnover. Germany, Malaysia, and some of the European countries define MSMEs on these twin criteria of employment and turnover.

IFC's definition of SME	Micro enterprise: Revenue of up to US$100,000
	Small enterprises: Sales between US$100,000 and US$3 million
	Medium enterprises: Sales between US$3 million and US$15 million

They also differ from global definitions such as the OECD's that define firm size according to employee numbers. Under such definitions, firms are generally much bigger: small firms are firms with 10-50 employees with turnover up to EUR10 million, medium with 50-250 employees with turnover up to EUR50 million. These also differ from the definition FIs use based on loan size/SME borrower needs.

The way they spread

Micro, small and medium enterprises and the small manufacturing enterprises have been the seedbeds of entrepreneurship in this country. Several *technopreneurs* sprang up with the forward and backward linkages provided by the large manufacturing sector, both in the public sector and private sector. The MSME sector has also provided the large enterprises trained and skilled manpower on their shop-floors. Capital incentives were extended in relation to the size of the enterprise. Once the thresholds were crossed, enterprises were setting up either new enterprises or associated enterprises in order to milk the incentives. Thus, horizontal growth instead of vertical growth occurred perpetuating the small to think small, remain small and argue for small. The distorted incentive systems that came in the way of small growing to medium and the medium growing to large are in the process of correction.

The beginning of 1980s saw a few changes in industrial policies. But it was the 1990s that really kickstarted changes post-liberalisation. Policymakers started thinking of loosening their hold in favour of market-led growth of enterprises. The year 2006 marked a watershed for MSMEs with the enactment of MSME Development Act. By introducing systems and automation in clearances followed by accountability for delays, several state governments have moved to facilitation from controls and unnecessary regulations. Trade distortions at the domestic and global levels that have also contributed to the disconnect in the global markets apart from low level skill sets are also in the process of correction, although the market access issues are still being debated in the WTO Forum.

Heterogeneity

The MSME sector in India is highly heterogeneous in terms of the size of the enterprises, variety of products and services produced, and the levels of technology employed. While at one end of the MSME spectrum there are highly innovative and high growth enterprises, around 94 per cent of MSMEs are unregistered, with a large number functioning in the informal or unorganised sector but contributing to 40 per cent of exports for over a decade. Besides the growth potential of the sector and its critical role in the manufacturing and value chains, the heterogeneity and the unorganised nature of the Indian MSMEs are important aspects that need to be factored into policy making and programme implementation. However, the small enterprise optimism is at its lowest level with the continuous decline in the growth of the manufacturing and infrastructure sectors, its springboard for growth.

While the size and economic diversity of India present several unique challenges to the role of the government in supporting MSME capacity and growth, the underlying challenges faced by India appear in no way unique when compared to an SME in almost any economy in the world.

3

MSME Business Environment and Challenges

The Industrial Environment and The Business Fit

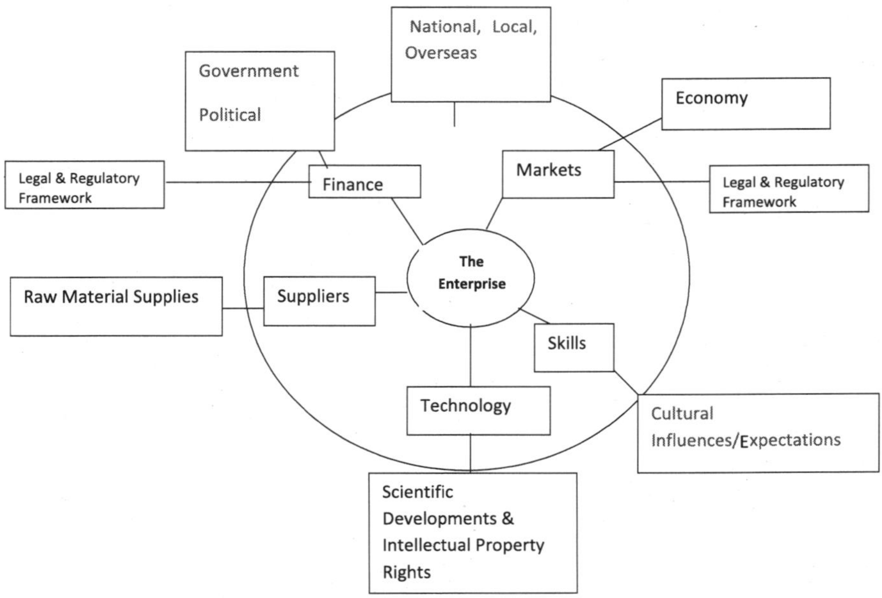

Whatever be the size and nature of an enterprise, it has to find a business fit in the industrial eco-system. Proprietor-led enterprises and small family partnerships still find difficulty in finding such a business fit. The complex regulations that govern their technologies, processes and products detailed in the above chart are the first challenge they face in their journey. And the most complex among them is access to 'finance'.

MSMEs, consequently, are facing many challenges due to internal and external factors that impact MSME performance.

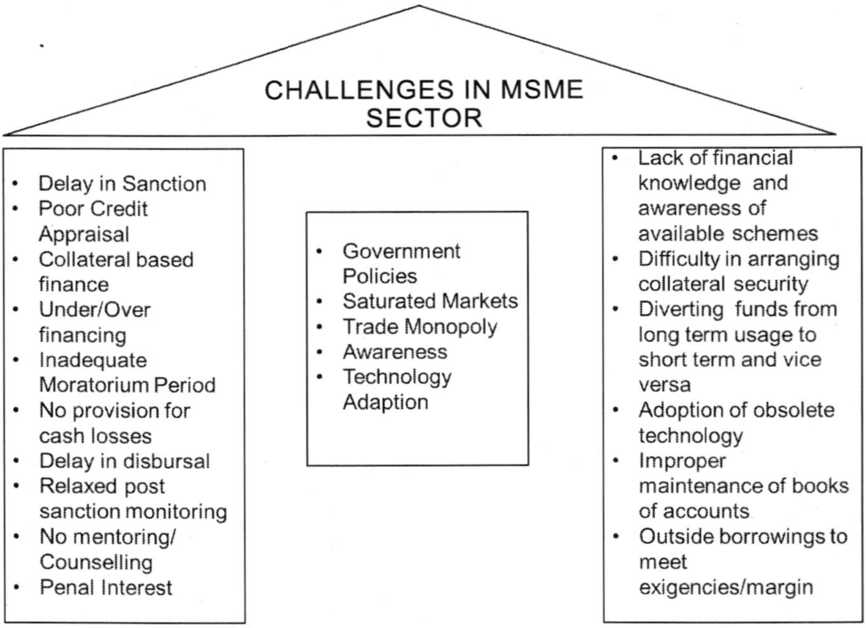

External challenges and issues include factors like changes in legal systems, estimating market conditions, environmental factors include political, legal, social and economic factors and socio, cultural and environmental factors which determine an entrepreneur's ability to become an entrepreneur.

Internal factors include all management-related factors like production, marketing, human resource development, financial and infrastructure-related factors, etc.

In considering both internal and external factors MSMEs can manage and control internal factors, but external factors can be removed by government involvement through implementing some specific schemes and programmes for respective sectors and also by category of industry. Internal challenges are production, marketing, financial, human resource development and infrastructure, etc. Production challenges include lack of power, lack of resources, lack of scarcity, lack of high cost raw materials, poor quality of raw materials, lack of machinery, etc. Marketing challenges include lack of promotional strategies, lack of market channels, lack of networking, lack of organised distribution channels, lack of delivery time, etc. Financial challenges include lack of credit from banks, lack of awareness on schemes and services, delayed process in bank, lack of working capital, etc.

Human resource development challenges include lack of training, lack of motivation among employees, lack of skilled employees, lack of technical and managerial training, improper way of recruiting etc. Infrastructure challenges include lack of water facilities, lack of storage facilities, lack of industrial facilities, lack of drainage facilities, etc.

External challenges arising out of the emerging environment need periodical strategic interventions from the entrepreneur, but internal challenges and issues can be overcome and are avoidable through certain safety measures and also through better management.

Size and growth of MSME market in India

Particulars	2018	2017	2016	2015	2014
MSME Sector contribution to GDP (%)	25	28.90	28.77	29.39	29.76
MSME Sector contribution to Indian Exports (%)	45	40	49.86	44.76	42.2
Banks Credit to MSE (manufacturing) (Rs bn)	3,730	3,697	3,715	3,800	3,517

Source: Annual Reports of the Ministry of MSMEs; and DIPP

Most micro and small enterprises (MSEs) miscalculate the demand and create excess capacities due to which they tend to become NPAs. While the case study of cold storages relates to 2003 such miscalculations of demand occur even now.

There has been no dearth of policies to assist the sector from the late 1970s till now involving the state governments, and other stakeholders, with public-private participation since the mid-1990s, industry and business associations. Still, the major issues centre around providing comfort for the start-ups for reducing regulatory delays through single window clearances, access to venture capital and private equity, differential treatment in labour welfare laws, supply of power uniformly and at affordable tariffs, credit at the right time in right measure, better payments and settlements between vendors and vendees and easy exit route.

Government of India has commenced the exercise of re-defining the SMEs to provide for vertical growth of the enterprise and lateral integration with the industrial eco-system in view of the changes in the climate for growth and ecological balance shifting to globalisation.

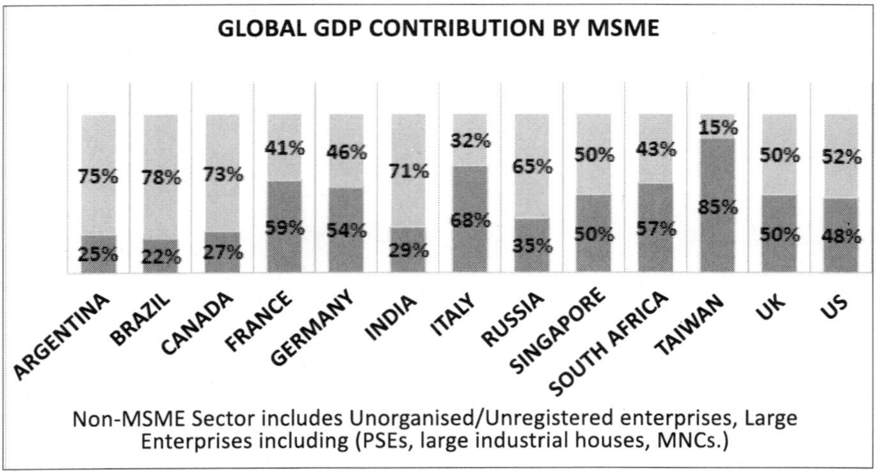

Source: RBI Annual Reports; Report on Trend and Progress of Banking in India by RBI. Official data for 2014-2015 FY not available.

Risks and Mitigation

The risks in MSME sector are multi-fold. We can broadly classify them as: Enterprise Risks, Entrepreneur Risks; Policy Risks; Operational Risks; Financial Risks or Credit Risks; Environmental Risks. Several of these risks overlap. In the context of globalisation, defining an enterprise as belonging to a particular category becomes important to access various services and facilities announced from time to time and networking arrangements.

Predicting MSME Risks – Models/Financials

SME failure rates are very often difficult to track properly. However, in the past few years, considerable research [e.g., Phillips and Kirchhoff (1989),[1] Watson and Everett (1993),[2] Watson & Everett (1996), Head (2003)] has been conducted to determine the rates and causes of such failures. Two of the principle reasons for unexpected closures are insufficient capitalisation and lack of planning. Several studies in India (Tewari Committee, 1985; Raju 1995, 2004) point to the following principal reasons for failure: unrealistic projected turnovers; reduction in capacity utilisation; excessive inventory pile up; erosion in margins; return of bills and cheques; lack of branding, poor marketing skills, lack of succession planning; absence of exit route; poor human relations management, improper maintenance of books of accounts; and casual approach to piling up arrears of loan instalments.

Some research studies note that 'when analysing business failure, it is extremely important to distinguish between failure and closure'. Watson and Everett, 1996[3] mention that closing firms could have been financially successful but closed down for other reasons: the sale of the firm or a personal decision by the owner to accept employment with another firm, to retire, or the like. To define failure, they created five categories: ceasing to exist (discontinuance for any reason); closing or a change in ownership; filing for bankruptcy; closing to limit losses; and failing to reach financial goals. Brian Headd (2003)[4] finds that only one-third of new businesses (33 per cent) closed under circumstances that owners considered unsuccessful.

'Risk management highlights the fact that the survival of a business entity depends heavily on its capabilities to anticipate and prepare for the change rather than waiting for the change to happen and then react to it. It should be clearly understood that the objective of risk management is not to prevent or prohibit taking risk, but to ensure that the risks are consciously taken with complete knowledge and clear understanding so that it can be measured to help in mitigation. It is more so in the case of SMEs.'(R.K. Raghavan, 2005)

The generic models proposed by many researchers to predict insolvency rely on profit and debt ratios that typically cannot be calculated for the large number of SMEs. Although the MSME Development and Regulation Act 2006 had a mandate to provide a framework for a safe exit for MSMEs, the effort is yet to see the light of the day. The TANSTIA-FNF (Tamil Nadu Small and Tiny Industries Association-Friedrich Naumann Foundation) Centre studied the issue at the instance of the Government of Tamil Nadu. Its Report basically suggests that wherever the entrepreneur's only dwelling house has been taken as collateral security while advancing credit to MSEs, such collateral security shall be exempt from any attachment by the financing institution unless the financing institution has evidence at its disposal that the dwelling house has been built with the finance provided to the enterprise. Despite significant debates on public-private partnership, MSMEs as a poverty reduction subject still haunts the minds of the policy makers and the wider public alike. This needs to undergo a change. A business case for MSME finance, first of all, needs to come to the minds of the public sector banks. Being the financial muscle of the government, a change in their mindset will help the mission of priority sector lending get translated into the interest of the MSMEs Policy Actions Needing Attention.

The following policy areas deserve consideration for MSME sector to become an effective instrument of inclusive growth:

(i) Merging the SFCs with SIDBI.
(ii) Merging the Technology Consultancy Organisations (TCOs) with state-level Entrepreneurship Development Institutions (EDIs).

(iii) Making SLBC into a professional body with greater authority.
(iv) Creation of a state-level MSME Factoring Fund to which banks can contribute.
(v) Setting up of MSME Financial Inclusion-cum-Growth Fund.
(vi) Setting up of local Economic Development Councils, with major role of banks, as in the UK.
(vii) State-level Small Business Finance Hubs – each hub to be managed by a bank.
(viii) Starting MSME Insurance, on lines of ECGC (Export Credit Guarantee Corporation of India).
(ix) Setting up of MSME Labour Bank.

Growth of the manufacturing sector is critical for achieving higher growth and human development. The younger generation looks for innovation and promising opportunities in manufacturing sector. The services sector that is close to peaking looks to the manufacturing sector for its sustained growth. MSMEs continue to influence the growth of the manufacturing sector.

No doubt any business entity needs robust risk management systems, but the MSMEs need much more than that as they may not have the wherewithal to manage and control risks due to their very size and other limitations. This is not true in the case of large corporate entities where professional personnel take care of many aspects pertaining to risk. All risk-taking units must operate within approved procedures, limits and controls. Certain misconceptions such as MSMEs may get low rating, provide unreliable information, may not afford the fees for getting them rated, etc. will have to be dispelled first. However, rating agencies with specialised teams with analytical tools customised to MSME sector will go a long way in putting in place the proper mechanism in this regard.

The Union Budget 2014-15 gave much needed attention to promoting entrepreneurship, providing equity and maintaining the eco-system of MSMEs as key to industrial development and sustained growth of the manufacturing sector, as could be noticed from the following proposals:

1. Creation of a corpus of Rs 10,000 crore for providing equity through Angel funds, Patient Capital, quasi-equity, soft loans and other risk capital will facilitate start-up companies.

2. Initial sum of Rs 100 crore for 'Start-up Village Entrepreneurship Programme' at the state level for encouraging rural youth to take up local entrepreneurship programmes.
3. Corpus of Rs 2000 crore to be set up to establish Technology Centre Network.
4. Development of an entrepreneur-friendly legal bankruptcy framework for SMEs that will enable easy exit.
5. To incentivise small entrepreneurs in the manufacturing sector, the government has also proposed to provide investment allowance at the rate of 15 per cent to a manufacturing company that invests more than Rs 25 crore in any year in new plant and machinery for investments up to 2016-17.
6. A nationwide 'District level Incubation and Accelerator Programme' to be taken up for incubation of new ideas and necessary support for accelerating entrepreneurship.

Successful execution of all these promises a significant boost for entrepreneurs and SMEs and facilitate the promotion and development and enhancing the economic growth of the country. This has potential for generating green shoots on an otherwise dry industrial landscape.

The efforts proved incomplete as facilitation centres at the district levels require coordinated efforts with state governments to scale up the efficiencies of the District Industries Centres and promoting Rural Industrial Parks. The need for Rural Industrial Parks (RIP) arises from the inability of the entrepreneurs to access land—one of the most important factors of production—due to competing demands and phenomenal growth of the real estate sector.

The Government would do well to establish RIPs with all amenities required for the micro and small enterprises and allocate land on long-term lease with the facility to mortgage leasehold rights to access institutional credit. Under PPP mode, the RIPs should also have primary health centres, schools up to class X and residential complex for workers. The entrepreneurs can have the option of owning the industrial site as and when they can afford it by paying the initial price of occupation. These RIPs would help to prevent migration of rural labour; provide social security and economic empowerment and growth of manufacturing sector.

The 'Make in India' initiative has no doubt given new direction to industry and entrepreneurship. The policy relaxations now target accelerated improvements in 'ease of doing business in India'; attracting more FDI investments in sectors hitherto treated with suspicion, like Defence and Aeronautics; fiscal benefits moving in tandem with the sector's emerging needs and creating a uniform tax code throughout the country with the introduction of goods and services tax (GST).

The constitution of a High-Level Committee by the RBI at the instance of Government of India gave the hope that the key issue of easing credit markets would also move in tandem so that domestic firms would be able to access credit competitively and also be in a position to tap international markets or foreign firms that have better access to capital in their home country. The skill sets are already on the radar for improvement with industries partnering the high-end technical and management education institutions. The hopes are high, and the efforts are at the beginning.

NO LONGER FISHING IN TROUBLED WATERS

Shrimp Meal

There was yet another case where a unit manufacturing shrimp head meal, poultry and fish ensilage as a partnership firm went into problems but was subsequently bailed out by the bank. The unit was sanctioned a composite term loan of Rs 10 lakh on 24 March 2001. There was delay in getting power connection which also led to delay in installation of machinery by 10 months. The commercial production, therefore, got delayed by one full year. This led to the unit becoming NPA even on the date of starting. This unit, located in Visakhapatnam, requested for replacement of the term loan by five years with payment of interest obligation up front. The zonal office considered this proposal favourably.

This was a case where incipient sickness was identified well in time and remedial action also taken by the financing institutions.

PROFILING THE RISKS

Enterprise risks

The entrepreneurs' choice of a lending institution plays a key role in furthering the growth of the enterprise. Some entrepreneurs choose an institution close to their location. Most entrepreneurs take the trouble of drawing up a road map for the enterprise for the next five to ten years and see which bank best suits their requirements.

The choice of a bank based on close affiliation to a political party or a neighbouring friendly branch manager or on the basis of proximity to the units or size of the branch or bank poses varying risks for sustainable financial institutional relationship.

Entrepreneurial risks

Entrepreneurial risks arise from the perceived knowledge levels required for the enterprise, qualifications, family background, egocentric issues, family relationships, relationships developed during the course of setting up and running the enterprise. Entrepreneurial risks could also be attributed to our educational system that is geared towards preparing people for employment and not towards developing entrepreneurship. As a result, those who do not secure jobs in the job markets move towards setting up enterprises, with the exception of family-based entrepreneurs.

Character and integrity, competence and attitude are the four attributes generally applied to judge entrepreneurial risks. The first two are subjective and mostly on-time assessment. An entrepreneur may be of excellent character and integrity and could also be coming from an excellent family known for such characteristics. But when the failure occurs either for want of money in time or when markets deceive him, there could be a prospect of his moving into the risk area of default. The usual probability analysis would not have captured such an eventuality.

There are entrepreneurs born; there are family-based entrepreneurs where they walk into the enterprise at some convenient stage in their career; there are failed graduates and technically qualified persons who fail to secure employment of their choice and start enterprises with a small amount of capital at their disposal and with confidence in their technology skills; they are also known as technopreneurs. Their location—rural, semi-urban, urban and metro—[5] determine their reach to the markets as also the nature and complexion of their products.

Some technopreneurs, overconfident of their technological capabilities, choose to go in for second hand machines with a view to squeezing oil out of sand. They simply do not realise that the seller of the second-hand technology moved to a higher level of technology to push a more cost-effective product into the market ahead of them. As a result, these entrepreneurs do not penetrate into new markets or new products. They end up as enterprises killed by the slow poison of incompetence, inefficiency and loss of reputation. The lending institution that reposed faith in the qualification and experience in technology alone in such technopreneurs pays a heavy price (Raju and Pujari, 2009: p. 35-37).

There are many entrepreneurs who do not possess knowledge of finance and do not maintain the required books of accounts and stocks properly or in a manner that the lender wants them to maintain. Recognising this need, some banks invest in educating the entrepreneurs through their own or collaborative training institutions and fill this gap. Some progressive banks have chosen to finance computerisation as part of the project cost when on-line access to information on stocks, debtors, creditors and capacity utilisation has insured the financing institution against the usual credit and marketing risks.

The pressure to produce results is great, given the volatility of the start-up environment and stakeholder impatience. Thus, start-up delivery units risk over-promising and underachieving. To minimise this possibility, initiatives should be based on estimated impact on start-up activity (usually measured by how much activity can be enhanced along the funnel from start-up creation to growth and maturity) and the feasibility of implementation (a more qualitative internal assessment). (Kirchherr, Scherf and Suder, 2014)

McKinsey' (2012) study of US small business succinctly observes, 'What's particularly disturbing is that the greatest decline in entrepreneurial activity occurred in the 18–24-year-old cohort. While older entrepreneurs bring more experience and a higher likelihood of success to their business building, the shortage of young business founders means that the US economy is currently not producing enough of its next generation of serial entrepreneurs.' Perhaps, it is equally valid in the case of Indian MSMEs, raising concerns about entrepreneurial education, development and training a national priority.

Environmental risks

An estimated 70 per cent of the total industrial pollution load is attributed to the Small and Medium Enterprises (SMEs) many of which, particularly the small-scale units, continue to use obsolete technologies with primitive or no pollution control methods. This is an issue which has been of concern to the industry associations also. CII Natural Capital Conservation and Development (NCCD) Council, in its key issues/directions,[6] calls for developing ways in which SMEs could be assisted to implement sustainability practices. A study of the environmental performance of Indian SMEs would reveal that a progressive framework or roadmap of environmental performance does not exist.[7] The existing assistance and financial schemes are to an extent piecemeal and uncoordinated and require integration into a well-thought-out framework. The accepted challenges to improving environmental compliance by SMEs can be stated as:

(i) The government's regulatory stand, reflected by its legislation, policies and procedures.
(ii) The challenge of Education and Awareness: The need for the businesses to understand and appreciate the degradation of the environment by their actions.
(iii) The third challenge is time. Time to start and the time for the actions to yield results. The lesser the time taken, the better.
(iv) The fourth challenge is cost. Funding compliance which in most cases is viewed as unproductive expenditure.

According to the Ministry of Environment and Forests (MOEF), SMEs account for 40 per cent of industrial production, employ limited pollution control technologies and are responsible for an estimated 70 per cent of the total industrial pollution load nationwide. Effective environmental enforcement requires informed consensus on environmental management objectives and policies that are based on a good understanding of the shared roles and responsibilities of all players, including the regulator, the regulated community (developers and polluters) and the affected community (general public).[8]

This fundamental notion of *shared responsibility* is currently challenged in India by the general perception among the public, project proponents, and development authorities alike that environmental ills are the sole responsibility of environmental agencies which fail to effectively implement and enforce the laws (WB 2006). As India's economy continues to accelerate, the performance of the environmental regulator will come under increased scrutiny and pressure.

To deal with these impacts, India has developed a comprehensive set of environmental laws and institutions, including a very active judiciary. A self-regulatory mechanism has been introduced.

Self-monitoring and reporting

According to the National Environmental (Protection) Rules of 1986, each polluting facility must submit an Environmental Statement at the end of each financial year (April through March). The Environmental Statement should include information relating to water, raw material consumption, air and water pollution discharged by globally accepted parameters hazardous waste generation and soil waste generation, its reuse, recycling and disposal and the pollution abatement measures.

Lack of reporting or false reporting may lead to criminal or administrative penalties. The existing legal framework, however, does not authorise enforcement actions through the courts based on self-disclosed reports. Rather, government agencies can only pursue legal action on the basis of "legal" samples taken by inspectors who are certified to conduct inspections in accordance with specified procedures. As a result, not using self-reported information is a significant constraint in promoting compliance and enforcement.

Marketing risks

Small entrepreneurs often suffer from both pricing and branding risks. This arises because of lack of comprehension of the risks in pricing the product hedging this risk. If marketing expenditure or advertisement expenditure or branding expenditure is treated as a part of working capital, the industry has potential to turn sick for it cannot realise these costs from the price of the product. It has to be spread over a number of years when the product acquires competitiveness in domestic and global markets. The entrepreneurs require professional expertise or hire professional expertise in framing a proposal to the banks seeking investment capital for these purposes.

Promotion through co-operative societies/public sector units and other professional marketing agencies would encourage better SME performance. Export promotion centres in the various clusters would be greatly advantageous to SMEs. The government and the several Export Promotion Councils should enable common display centres for SME products at strategic locations and conduct frequent Trade Fairs abroad. The limited resources of MSMEs have to be pooled for collective displays in the domestic and global markets. Indian brands should command the market both in terms of quality and price. Ministry of MSME extends market access support through grant and participation assistance.

Although in most discussions on small enterprise development, finance comes up as a key issue, it is often confined to one area, adequacy of credit. It is time to move away from adequacy to other aspects of credit, such as timeliness, uses of credit and appropriateness of financial products. Between micro finance and venture capital, there are much more issues that need to be debated. Such a debate implies not only enhanced flow of credit, but also, more business for financial institutions. Equity related products like those in small businesses of the US need exploration keeping the behavioural dynamics of Indian entrepreneurs. While the problems related to risk aversion and the solutions to address credit risk management for these clients have never been provided through appropriate externalities, as the elbow room for banks to do due diligence and extension is getting extremely restricted. It is important to understand why the banks that cry themselves hoarse on MSMEs as high-risk prone are not picking up the institutional guarantee mechanism created through the CGTMSE (Credit Guarantee Fund Trust for Micro and Small Enterprises) in full measure.

Environmental Impact Assessment necessary for several sectors has also become a casualty. Insurance of the units' assets as part of the credit dispensation mechanism takes place more by default. It is not uncommon that the renewals take place mechanically and not by scrutiny. It is realised that the insurance falls short of the requirement only when a calamity occurs, Checks and balances have become too mechanical and lost relevance. The size of an enterprise does not provide insurance against the environmental risks. Take for example the Tirupur hosiery industry that was generating exports of the order of Rs 5000 crore per annum and there are nearly 20 bank branches in that small town. Yet the pollution the industry caused necessitated stringent measures from the government leading to their closure. The slurry generated while dyeing the yarn and the requirements of water have left the industry in the lurch. The industry that was an icon in Tamil Nadu is today in doldrums. Environmental risks have to be envisioned and hedged properly with the required investments and these could be of long-term nature and should be of the nature of term loan and not working capital.

RISK MITIGATION MEASURES

More recently the RBI has called upon banks to set up financial management advisory desks to help MSMEs with non-core functions such as accounting, taxation and financial management. Banks could charge a reasonable fee to provide these services to the enterprises. According to the Central Bank, the top management of banks should show their commitment to the MSME sector by clearly spelling out the targets for expanding the MSME portfolio at the branch level and closely monitoring them. Further, to ensure transparency, banks should disclose the interest rates they charge their borrowers segment-wise in the balance sheets. Despite the wide-ranging discussions on Business Development Services (BDS) following the Donor Committee Report (2004),[9] there are several cultural factors in India that hold back the development of BDS markets in the country. These factors need to be overcome.

All these would demand that banks should tighten their credit appraisal standards. They should not relax their standards just because credit guarantee institutions such as the CGTMSE and the ECGC will pick up the tab if loans go bad. A pro-active policy would imply that entrepreneurs should be encouraged to experiment with business ideas. If the entrepreneurs fail in their ventures, they should have an easy exit policy.

Notes

1. Bruce D. Phillips and Bruce A. Kirchhoff, "Formation, Growth and Survival; Small Firm Dynamics in the U.S. Economy," *Small Business Economics*, Vol. 1, Issue 1, 1989, http://papers.ssrn. com/sol3/papers.cfm?abstract_id=1504489
2. John Watson and Jim Everett, "Defining Small Business failure," International *Small Business Journal*, Vol. 11, Issue No. 3, 1993.
3. John Watson and Jim E. Everett, "Do Small Businesses have high failure rates? Evidence from Australian retailers," *Journal of Small Business Management*, 34, September 1996, pp. 45-62, https://www.researchgate.net/publication/285013499_Do_small_businesses_have_high_failure_rates_Evidence_from_Australian_retailers/citation/download
4. Brian Headd, "Redefining Business Success: Distinguishing Between Closure and Failure," *Small Business Economics*, Vol. 21, No. 1, 2003, pp. 51-61.
5. Rural, semi-urban, urban and metro classification is population centric and the terms are akin to the Census of India.
6. http://www.govtindustry-environment.com/industryspeak-main.asp?id
7. OECD 2006. Environmental Compliance and Enforcement in India: Rapid Assessment. Jointly produced by OECD and the Secretariat of the Asian Environmental Compliance and Enforcement Network (AECEN) under the OECD Programme of Environmental Co-operation with Asia.
8. Source: www.moef.nic.in
9. Donor Committee Report, GTZ. *www2.gtz.de/wbf/4tDx9kw63gma/White_business-env.doc*

4

MSME Sector: Policy Environment

If public policy till the beginning of this century is based on imagination and aspiration, it is now based on information and competition. Destiny is decided not just by past actions so much as the demands of the future. This may sound axiomatic but it should be guiding the policy for MSME sector, a daunting task indeed. MSME development, seen as integral element is not *sui generis* subject matter. The sector can prosper in a healthy climate and conducive policy environment.

This chapter intends to provide a brief review of the MSME sector policies thus far in terms of where we are, where we intend to go and what should be done to realise our intentions, particularly in the global environment.

EVOLUTIONARY PROCESS

Policy Framework

The pre-independent Indian economy had a widespread presence of rural and cottage industries and artisans. These were dependent mostly on local resources and local markets. The skills in most cases were inherited. It was only during the 1950-70 period that the growth of small industry sector occurred.

The promotion of the small-scale sector in India has been an important thrust of industrial policy since Independence though the focus of concern changed with the priorities of each Five-Year Plan. The six Industrial Policy Resolutions, which have been framed since 1948 have set out the guidelines for the country's industrial development with different degrees of emphasis on the main objectives. The Industries Development and Regulation Act of 1951, as mentioned earlier, provided the basic framework for the post-Independence industrialisation strategy. Since the model for industrialisation in the 1950s was based on capital-intensive heavy industries, the priority of employment generation required the development of widely dispersed, mass consumption-good producing, labour-intensive, small-scale industries.

As the process of economic development led to changing priorities, the policy focus shifted to regional imbalances (1977), ancillarisation (1980), exports and dispersal in rural areas (1990) and then to Small, Tiny and Village Industries (1991). However, the entire industrial activity was controlled by the industrial licensing system; trade and foreign investments also had similar controls at the entry point. In order to encourage growth of small industries as supportive to large public enterprises in general, and to correct regional imbalances in industrial growth, subsidies, concessions, and government support started flowing in. Therefore, the so-called protective policies of the Government of India in favour of small industries were a consequence and not a cause of their growth. As could be observed from the analysis that follows, the SSI sector has grown to a stage of substantial presence in the economy. Anachronistically, even when there was deceleration in the large industry, the small industry is reported to have registered a comparatively higher growth. This is perhaps the most compelling reason for the Expert Committee on Small Enterprises to state: 'Small-scale enterprises will continue to need exceptional support in terms of financial resources, technological development and infrastructure.' (Abid Hussain Committee Report, 1997; 21) These types of supports, it is to be noted, are compatible with the provisions of the WTO agreement. This chapter intends to provide a brief review of the MSME sector policies thus far in terms of where we are, where we intend to go and what should be done to realise our intentions, particularly in the global environment.

The Nation on The Rise

Jamie Dimon, Chairman of J.P. Morgan, in an interview to *The Economic Times*[1] said: 'India is growing at 7 per cent plus, the deficit has gone down quite a bit and the government has made changes which are conducive to future growth.' It is now an acknowledged fact that the next decade would see India as the driving force of global economic growth. Such attestation demands that all the policies that drive growth should be in sync with each other. Micro, Small and Medium Enterprises have acquired the niche as engine of industrial growth and enable exports look northwards.

MSMEs in India continue to draw the attention of both the Union and state governments due to their ability to contribute to the job-enhancing growth of the economy and export potential with their presence in more than 6000 products. These products cover 58.5 million establishments of which about 77.6 per cent are engaged in non-agricultural activities (excluding public administration, defence and compulsory social security activities) with 89.8 per cent as own enterprises (with only owner as employee)[2] and 11-12 per cent contribution to the GDP. This is what that makes the policy formulation indeed daunting. Continuing fiscal stress due to competing demands on the Nation State from several sectors, particularly, infrastructure and minimal government restrict the ability of the nation to give subsidies and concessions however much the sector deserves both for sustenance and growth.

MSME Development Act 2006 provides the legal support to the policy framework. The Act seeks to facilitate the development of these enterprises as also enhance their competitiveness. It also provides for a statutory consultative mechanism at the national level with balanced representation level of all the stakeholders with a wide range of advisory services as mentioned in the Ministry's website. MSME Ministry will play a supplementary role with project support for employment promotion, entrepreneurship development, and livelihood promotion. The project and support system as a policy offshoot is detailed out in Annexure-1.

India's manufacturing sector contributes about 16 per cent to the GDP, and India's share in world manufacturing is only 1.8 per cent. This is in stark contrast to China; where manufacturing contributes 34 per cent to the GDP with a 13.7 per cent share in world manufacturing—up from 2. 9 per cent in 1991. (Planning Commission, 2012)

With changing global realities, the manufacturing sector will need to be the bulwark of employment creation over the next decade, in contrast to current employment of only 9 per cent of India's working population. India's demographic dividend can only then be sufficiently exploited through the systematic growth of this sector.

The World Economic Forum in its latest report has ranked India 37 among 138 nations that responded to the survey of Global Competitiveness Report 2016-17.

Business Confidence Index in India increased to 57.20 in the second quarter of 2016 from 54.10 in the first quarter of 2016. Business Confidence in India averaged 57.95 from 2005 until 2016, reaching an all-time high of 71.80 in the first quarter of 2007 and a record low of 45.70 in the third quarter of 2013. A score above 50 indicates positive confidence while a score above 75 would indicate strong positive confidence.

Doing Business in India 2016 Report of the World Bank places India at 130 rank among 189 nations, up from 147 in 2014.

During the 12th Five Year Plan, the Integrated Skill Development Scheme targeted to train 26.75 lakh persons in all the sub-sectors of the textile sector, such as textiles (both technical and traditional); apparel; handlooms; jute, silk and wool; handicrafts Government of India had also set up a Rs 100-crore venture capital fund to provide equity support to start-ups in the textile sector in order to encourage innovation in this export intensive sector. It has also allotted Rs 700 crore for the development of technical textiles where the annual growth is likely to be around 3.5 per cent.

India Inc. in its interaction with Prime Minister on 'Make in India' campaign highlighted a few important factors to be addressed with a sense of urgency that include building up of critical infrastructure across the country supported by stable policies, a transparent and competitive tax and duty structure, efficient and time-bound administration through e-governance, cost-effective and reliable energy coupled with logistics in order that India becomes globally competitive in the manufacturing arena.

'Large units tend to break up into smaller units.' (Schumacher, 1973; p. 52) But, today, the mergers, acquisitions and joint ventures are only an effort to demonstrate the urge for becoming big/gigantic to gain what economists call 'economies of scale'. Yet, as soon as great size has been created, there is often a tendency – rather a 'strenuous attempt to attain smallness within bigness' (Ibid; 53). British National Coal Board, once a monolith, was transformed into 'well-coordinated assembly of lively, semi-autonomous units, each with its own drive and sense of achievement'. The footloose characteristic of the micro and small enterprises gives the enormous scope for their spread to backward areas.

Innovation in manufacturing

Innovation in manufacturing fosters economic development and creates employment. But it needs to be channelled, encouraged and protected. The way forward for the country is to encourage investments in research and development, protection of intellectual property rights and financing of incubation centres. The eco-system of innovation requires certain essentialities to be in place: a strong scientific and technological base; investment from both public and private sectors and innovation. While cost arbitrage has formed the lynchpin of outsourcing in this area for long time, it is time for the paradigm shift to 'strategic innovation' where talent development takes the front seat. Innovation inevitably carries with it the risk that not every creative idea will be commercially viable, and therefore fiscal incentives like China, South Korea, and Japan etc., would seem a better option than financial incentives for sustained growth of this sector.

Global environment for SMEs is influenced by growth seen in employment generation, innovation and technology. The word Micro unlike in India is not part of the SME policy syndrome. Compatibility issues naturally arise viewed in the context of competitiveness of the sector. Knowledge driven global enterprises are devoting their attention to innovation, research and development as key to their sustainability and growth.

STRONG ROOTS ON WEAK SOIL

There was the case of a manufacturer of edible cutlery, an innovative product financed by Bank of India.

The firm was in the name of a lady entrepreneur though it was the husband, the key entrepreneur, who runs the unit and right from the design of the machinery it was he who was in constant touch with the operations. This obsession with research blinded him to the market potential. He expected the market to just grab this product. The process involved baking of dough made of jowar, bajra flour and using various moulds to turn them into edible cutlery of various shapes – like spoons of various shapes and sizes, fork, chop sticks, etc. 'Eat with spoon and eat the spoon too', epitomises his product profile. The key entrepreneur was a retired scientist from ICRWASAT and does not know even a bit of finance and marketing. He was ambitious and less of a listener.

The key entrepreneur availed finance from Bank of Maharashtra three years before approaching the Bank of India in the name of his wife. He was deceived by the partners and the account became NPA. The transaction was a victim of a fraud by an employee and, therefore, the case with Bank of Maharashtra was in limbo. This fact was not disclosed to the Bank of India as the unit was a proprietrix unit. After detailed discussions for over a week the facts have been unraveled. While this may not have any impact on the progress of the unit's functioning with Bank of India, the latter's due diligence exercise suffered to that extent.

Punch line: This enterprise took to crowd funding and indulged in risky marketing. Its financial indiscipline landed the entrepreneur in jail in 2019. Bank of India has financed working capital of Rs 10 lakh with credit guarantee trust fund support and term loan backed up with collateral security. There would appear to have been no discussion with the entrepreneur's post sanction. Even when the unit defaulted on submission of stock statements and financial data annually, except bank sending routine reminders the bank did not appear to have evinced interest in looking at what was happening to the unit.

When the unit wanted to relocate the unit from Cherlapally to LB Nagar, a non-industrial area, the permission was granted. Post-shifting, the bank officials did not visit even once to look at their assets.

Faced with losses and property acquisition notice, the entrepreneur approached the state level Inter Institutional Committee to argue its case for postponing the auction and giving him time to start repayment. This was the first time that the unit approached the Industries Department.

The Department's consultant has struggled to put the entrepreneurs on track that included opening up for discussions on marketing strategies, packing and forwarding the products, and guiding him in finance. A strategic partner, Growth Idea Lab, came forward to provide bridge finance to bail out of the NPA status provided the bank was willing for rehabilitation. There were discussions even with the regulators.

Even in this case, the actual facts have not been brought to the notice during the SLIIC committee meeting: The unit was allowed working capital, and use for research and development. This has happened because the Bank officials did not at all visit the unit after the first sanction was made. Pre-sanction visit was the only visit. The Bank failed to follow up and guide the unit properly ever since it was set up. This has happened because they had adequate collateral security at their command. Even as the unit was being interviewed by the *CNN IBN*, an acquisition notice under SAFRAESI was slapped on the flat – Rs 1 crore value of security against the outstanding of Rs 83 lakh (Rs 65 lakh plus interest Rs 28 lakh).

In both the cases both the banks failed to follow the RBI guidelines on rehabilitation and revival of sick enterprises: There was neither a corrective action plan, nor handholding nor a TEV study. Several facts are not disclosed by the banks at the SLIIC making a mockery of the forum.

During the course of revival, the entrepreneur-initiated marketing through Café Coffee Day with a good sample order. Packaging the product has also been changed insulating it from breakages in transit. He went on social marketing with a presentation on YouTube and this has become viral. Crowd funding flowed to the unit. The unit did not HAVE TO turn back. Though the revival happened despite the bank, three years later, lack of financial discipline and greed landed him in jail.

Notes

1. M.C. Govardhana Rangan and Saloni Shukla, "Not an Exaggeration to Call India Sole Bright Spot," *The Economic Times*, 19 September 2016, P 1, https://economictimes.indiatimes.com/markets/expert-view/not-an-exaggeration-to-call-india-sole-bright-spot-jpmorgan-chairman-jamie-dimon/articleshow/54398435.cms?from=mdr
2. Sixth Economic Census, Ministry of Statistics and Programme Implementation, Government of India, 2016

5

Future Lies Here: Sub-sector Outlook

The CII Report (2019) reveals the strength of the sector in job creation, yet again. Over the four years (2014-18) MSMEs witnessed a growth of 13.9 per cent. Micro firms created the largest number of jobs and are expected to continue the trend for the next three years, the Report noted. During the period, Maharashtra, Gujarat and Telangana were the largest job generators, while Maharashtra, Tamil Nadu and Telangana were the top three states in case of exporters. The future of the economy obviously lies here if we were to care for job-oriented growth.[1]

The MSME sector, as noted earlier, contributes more than 6,000 products. Predominant among them are Engineering and Fabrication, Auto Components, Food Processing, Electronics Equipment, Textiles (handlooms, power looms, knitwear and apparel and garment manufacturing) and Defence equipment and components. This chapter highlights some of the features of these sub-sectors. As data related to each of these sectors is in unreliable space, analysis is restricted to qualitative aspects in brief. Since Defence equipment and components has been opened up only during 2017-18, no meaningful analysis would be possible. Although gems and jewellery have a significant contribution in the MSME exports, no analysis has been proposed due to its volatility and concentration only in a few states like Gujarat, Maharashtra and Tamil Nadu.

Engineering and Fabrication

Engineering and Fabrication sub-sector occupies a large space in the MSME sector—particularly in some clusters like Jamshedpur, Peenya (Bengaluru), Cherlapalli, Mallapur, Sanatnagar, Jeedimetla (Telangana), BHPV Industrial Estate, SEZ (Visakhapatnam), Kalinganagar (Jajpur District, Odisha), Cuttack, etc. Most of the enterprises came up as ancillaries to major industries like the TATA group, Visakhapatnam Steel Plant, Bharat Heavy Plate and Vessels, Hindustan Machine Tools. Post-liberalisation, these enterprises widened their markets both within and outside the country. The National Manufacturing Policy buttressed by 'Make in India' gave further impetus to this sub-sector.

Most of the units in such clusters/groups have the proximity of a few or all of the required raw materials: iron ore, coal, mica, bauxite, copper, aluminium, fire clay, graphite, kainite, sillimanite, lime stone, uranium, etc and collectivisation of requirements enhance the bargaining power of the units to secure raw materials at lesser cost than the isolated units.

The sector, however, suffers from lack of any significant research and development efforts. Most of the enterprises have low profitability as most of them are subject to rate contracts which inhibit passing on the burden of increasing costs to the consumer. Volatility in steel prices impacts their production plans significantly. In spite of Skill Development Programmes, lack of skilled labour has been cited as a serious impediment for the growth of this sub-sector. Some of the enterprises outside the clusters or SEZs suffer the additional disadvantages as several of them are sub-contracting firms to the rate contracted enterprises. High power tariffs, in some parts of the country, low voltage and frequent interruptions in supply add to their troubles.

Credit risks for the sector emanate from the following factors:

- ❖ High dependence on profligate customers;
- ❖ Limited geographical diversity of markets;

- Cyclical demand;
- Obsolete technology;
- Volatile raw material prices;
- Inflexible pricing;
- Shortage of skilled labour; and
- Inadequate physical infrastructure.

Ability of the banks to service the MSMEs – in fact, micro units will be far and few – depends on the transaction costs, efficient recovery process, and available security. Though repetitive, extended CGTMSE guarantee cover up to Rs 2 crore per enterprise, particularly in clusters/ SEZs, should actually incentivise and accelerate lending aided by this risk mitigating tool.

The Report of the RBI Working Group on Flow of Credit to SSI sector, 2004 suggested adoption of the **4-C approach: Customer focus, Cost control, Cross-sell and Contain risk.** In the context of increasing pressure on banks to lend responsibly and adequately as also in time, banks would do well to extend credit in clusters and industrial estates/industrial parks and SEZs, that would reduce information asymmetry, provide better inter-firm comparison, and render cost-effective monitoring of the credit.

Auto Components

This sub-sector is the fastest growing one in the Indian economy and is the largest contributor to the exports in the MSME space. This sector has been growing at about 30 per cent per annum during the decade 2005-15. The advantage of the sector is that production process can be disintegrated and tiered. PSBs are the major lenders for this sector. This sector is present in 18 states although Tamil Nadu, Uttar Pradesh, Madhya Pradesh, Punjab, Haryana, Maharashtra and West Bengal occupy more than 50 per cent of the MSME space. According to a Dun & Bradstreet study (2004) for SMERA (SME Rating Agency of India), 77 per cent constitute proprietary firms and 55 per cent partnership firms are suppliers to the OEMs and the replacement market. Almost 67 per cent of the firms are exporters. Around 16 per cent of the companies manufacture engine parts, 17 per cent manufacture body and chassis parts, 13 per cent suspension and braking parts, and 14 per cent manufacture drive transmission and steering parts. Only 35 per cent of the companies sell under a brand name and only 11 per cent have entered into joint ventures or collaborations either with domestic or international companies.

Poor infrastructure and lack of institutional assistance were cited as key hindrances to growth of these MSMEs. Delayed payments have been worrying these enterprises and the recently introduced TradEx, GeMs (Government e-Marketplace), and amendments to the MSE Facilitation Council functioning could reduce worries on this count. The IBC Code ensures quick exit of uneconomic enterprises.

Food Processing Sector

The food processing sector, often referred to as sunrise sector, has immense potential to transform the rural landscape of India by improving the value addition to the farm produce at or near the farm stead. An extensive and highly fragmented industry, it largely comprises of the following sub-segments: fruits and vegetables; milk and milk products; beer and alcoholic beverages; meat and poultry; marine products; grain processing; packaged and convenience foods and packaged drinks. Constituting large numbers, they are mostly in unorganised MSME portfolio. This segment accounts for more than 70 per cent of the output in volume and 50 per cent in value terms. The organised sector has also been growing rapidly during the last 10 years. India ranks first in milk production and second in fruits and vegetables in the world.

India was ranked 12th in the world, in exports of food and food products in 2015. Major industries constituting the food processing sector are grain milling, sugar, edible oils, beverages, fruits and vegetables processing and dairy products. The contribution of the food processing sector to the Gross Value Addition (GVA) in 2014-15 amounted to US$22 billion at 2011-12 prices. In 2014-15, GVA in food processing grew by 5.78 per cent. The share of Food Processing Sector in GVA of manufacturing sector was 8.6 per cent in 2014-15.

Investment in fixed Capital in registered food processing sector grew from US$24.5 billion in 2012-13 to US$25.85 billion in 2013-14, at a growth rate of 6 per cent. The number of registered food processing units increased from 37,175 in 2012-13 to 37,445 in 2013-14. The food processing industry is one of the major employment intensive segments, contributing 11.69 per cent of employment generated in all Registered Factory sector in 2013-14. Exports have been steadily rising to 2 per cent and over during 2017.

Growth Drivers

- Liberalisation and the growth of organised retail has made the Indian market more attractive for global players; with a large agricultural resource base, abundant livestock and cost competitiveness, India is fast emerging as a sourcing hub of processed foods
- With a population size of 1.22 billion of which 604 million were under the age of 24 years in 2011, this rising youth population is likely to increase India's overall food consumption.
- Rising income levels, affluence and a growing middleclass.
- One-third of the population will be living in urban areas by 2020.
- Increasing desire for branded food as well as increased spending power.
- Large distinct consumer segments to support customised offerings/new categories and brands within each segment.
- Consumption in India is driven towards packaged and ready-to-eat foods.
- Favourable economic and cultural transformation, shift in attitudes and lifestyles, consumers are experimenting with different cuisines, tastes and new brands. There is an increase in awareness and concern for wellness and health, high protein, low fat, wholegrain and organic food.
- Exports of food items have been increasing steadily, the main export destinations being the Middle East and South East Asia.

A few states like Telangana have formulated a Food Processing Policy in 2018 to give boost to the Food Processing sector.

Electronics Equipment Production

Electronics equipment production has been growing steadily with CAGR of over 26 per cent in 2016. Its share in 2015 was 5 per cent of manufacturing. Most global firms have opened their manufacturing spaces or assembly lines in India – e.g., Samsung, Micromax, Foxcon, Motorola, LG, Ericson, Jabil Circuits, HP, Dell, Lenovo, HCL, Zenith, etc. Nokia that had its largest manufacturing unit in Tamil Nadu but shut shop a few years ago, is likely to come back with the firm re-entering the electronic manufacturing space.

In 2012, US-based management consulting firm Booz & Co reported that India would account for only three (3) percent of the global market by 2020, therefore self-reliance was not a viable tool to drive the globally competitive economies of scale. The Booz & Co study was sponsored by the Cellular Operators Association of India (COAI). According to the Telecom Equipment Manufacturers' Association of India (TEMA), contrary to the Government of India's thought process, the report seemed to conclude that there was not much scope for the Indian Telecom Equipment Manufactures in the current world scenario.

TEMA communication to the Honorable Minister of Communication said that "the telecom equipment market is expected to grow to US$40 billion by the year 2020, up from current level of US$10 billion and is an attractive proposition for the current foreign equipment suppliers to discourage home grown telecom equipment manufacturers.[2]

The main reasons for such growth are the size of market, liberal reforms in foreign direct investment, and the rationalisation of duty structure. In addition, the GST reform is set to accelerate growth of this organised segment.

Most PC vendors scout for component manufacturers outside the country such as Malaysia, China, Thailand, Vietnam, Czech Republic and Latin America. Manufacturing operations are not limited to PCs like HP in Uttarakhand and Dell in Tamil Nadu. Assembly lines have been set up in peripherals also – e.g., HP for Printers – inkjet and laser printers.

Both technology and telecom space in India is giving stiff competition to China, the traditional stronghold.

Credit to these sectors on easy and preferential terms holds the key to growth. Banks bitten by the NPA bug are still not able to see the prospects ahead in the manufacturing MSME space.

Textiles and Handicrafts

Next to agriculture, textiles sector is the largest employer. In so far as MSMEs are concerned, they have almost a dedicated space in handlooms, power looms, apparel and knitwear, and garmenting across cotton, silk and jute bases. The Ministry of Textiles has introduced a number of schemes to promote both domestic and export markets. A few of them relevant for the MSMEs are dealt with in this section.

The textiles sector employs close to 45 million people going by the Ministry of Textiles website information. By 2022, another 17 million would be added to the textile work force. Between 2014 and 2018, Integrated Skill Development Scheme—an employment-linked programme—trained 8.5 lakh persons in partnership with 58 government and industry partners. Handloom Brand image is on its way with zero-defect-zero-effect (on environment) providing assurance to consumers of genuineness and quality. MUDRA loans and RuPay cards are issued to handloom weavers at a concessional rate of interest of 6 per cent p.a. e-Marketing has generated Rs 21.25 crore as at the end of March 2019. Yarn worth Rs 130.56 crore was reported through dedicated eDhaga App. Hastakarga Samvardhan Sahayata Yojana was launched to support trained weavers with 90 per cent subsidy on looms/accessories. Besides, 381 new block/Mandal level clusters were sanctioned during 2014-18 with an outlay of Rs 502.77 crore of which Rs 186.85 crore was released.

With regard to power looms, in-situ upgradation of plain power looms was taken up during 2014-18 and 2.67 lakh looms have been upgraded under the scheme. Additional subsidy for rapier-kits was also given. PowerTex India was launched with a three-year time-frame involving an outlay of Rs 487 crore. It has nine components that include MUDRA loan for power looms up to Rs 20 lakh at subsidised rates. The Integrated Processing Development Scheme has been revised to provide assistance up to 50 per cent of the project cost—with a ceiling of Rs 75 crore—to industry clusters for setting up Common Effluent Treatment Plants with zero liquid discharge technology.

Handicrafts

Special projects for integrated development of handicrafts have been launched in Jharkhand, Uttarakhand, Kerala, Madhya Pradesh, Tamil Nadu, Andhra Pradesh, Telangana, Karnataka and Uttar Pradesh. Exports from handicrafts have increased by 35 per cent in 2014 to Rs 22,916 crore in 2018. Support through supply of tool kits and marketing is provided to craftspersons.

However, the data sheet available on the Ministry website is updated till 2012 only. Since much water has flown during the years 2012-18, an analysis is considered not appropriate.

Notes

1. "Massive job creation in small businesses; MSME job growth at 14% in last 4 years," Financial Express, 8 March 2019, https://www.financialexpress.com/economy/massive-job-creation-in-small-businesses-msme-job-growth-at-14-in-last-4-years/1509542/
2. "TEMA refutes Booz & Co Report on Indian Telecom Manufacturing," *Business Wire India*, 17 May 2012, https://www.businesswireindia.com/tema-refutes-booz-co-report-on-indian-telecom-manufacturing-31235.html

6

New Initiatives and Old Institutions

The Ministry of Micro, Small and Medium Enterprises is committed to strengthening the MSME sector to enable it remain competitive in a market-led growing economy and generate additional employment opportunities. Its endeavour is to provide the MSMEs proper and timely inputs:

- Adequate and timely credit – an unending effort;
- Funds for technology upgradation and modernisation;
- Adequate infrastructure facilities;
- Modern testing facilities and quality certification laboratories;
- Modern management practices and skill upgradation and training;
- Marketing assistance;
- Level playing field with the large enterprises;
- Close coordination with the state governments.

A few schemes like MUDRA, TradEX, GeMs, capital subsidy, and guarantee extension up to Rs 2 crore from CGTMSE launched during the last five years are proposed for review in this chapter.

The AMEX Bank Report (2017) of global SMEs relevant for Indian MSMEs highlights the following concerns:

- Cost of funds as the pain point
- Enterprises scaling up opportunities are not cognizable.
- Public procurement
- Competitive factors of markets
- Cost of social security
- Populist announcements
- Absence of plug-and-play facilities for manufacturing enterprises
- Trade-off of Climate Change
- Economic and Industrial Policies
- Knowledge facilitation

In Mexico, for example, there are 100 unions of SM enterprises to tackle the delayed payments and cash flow problems.

Keeping the job creation potential of SMEs in view, how can we create 100 million SMEs to **spawn growth**?

In the Finance Space:

- Culture of dependency has to change to self-reliance mechanism.
- Public sector and government departments have to pay within 15 days of receipt of goods invoiced and dispatched. Failure to do so should attract on-line penalties and downgraded rating.
- HR systems as of today are not able to attract smart people and retain them. Skill development should move in tandem with the requirements of this sector and frequent interface with grassroots institutions like the polytechnics, ITIs, etc would speed up the process.
- In a knowledge-based economy, reskilling and upskilling strategies have to evolve within the capabilities of the SMEs: how to support the environment for such ecosystem, what should the governments do?
- Clusters: While there are 1500 clusters, identify those that have agglomeration effect on growth and create conditions for replication.

Agencies and institutions for the development of the MSME sector have been designed to suit the specific policies. NGOs are also active in promoting MSME growth, with Japan having the largest number of such NGOs. These organisations include cooperatives, industry associations, chambers of commerce and industry and similar bodies. They are active mainly in providing much needed information on marketing and technological change. District Industries Centres (DICs) constitute an important component of the government's institutional framework at the grassroots level. As many as 12 ministries at the Union government have schemes in MSME space. Most important among them are textiles, defence, aeronautics, electronics, food processing, and skill building. Entrepreneurs are, however, disappointed with the functioning of the DICs.

Cast Alloys

Subba Rao, a highly qualified US-returned Engineer-cum-Management Graduate, began manufacture of Steel Strips, Special Alloy Steel & Iron Castings, by name Cast Alloys in January 1983 but the unit became defunct by 19 September the same year. With limits of around Rs 65 lakh, he was anxious to down the shutters mainly because of frustration with government officials.

There was a subsisting dispute with Sales Tax authorities on categorisation of these products. The unit's contention was that the wrong categorisation is responsible for the raising of a demand on him for Rs 50 lakh. He was also sore with the Electricity Department for the highest Power tariff that exists nowhere in the world. He mentioned that he did not have any problem with his bankers.

New Developments

The definition of MSMEs is set to change.

Tax rates: In anticipation of these revised definitions, the income tax rates of firms with turnover rates below Rs 250 crore have been reduced from 30 per cent to 25 per cent, (Finance Act, 2018).

Courts: As part of the ongoing business reforms action plan initiative, the definition of commercial courts in the 'Commercial Courts, Commercial Divisions and Commercial Appellate Divisions Act, 2015' was amended on 1 May 2018. The amendment allows commercial cases with a specified value of Rs 3.5 lakh upwards to be tried in commercial courts, as opposed to a floor of Rs 1 crore earlier. It is expected that this may assist in ensuring faster disposal of cases of small value, which are the kind of cases generally filed by MSMEs.

Goods and Services Tax (GST), an indirect tax, was introduced in India on 1 July 2017 and was applicable throughout the country. GST is likely to make compliance much easier and, therefore, encourage a wider section of enterprises to comply with the provisions.

EXISTING SCHEMES AVAILABLE FOR MSME SECTOR

Credit Guarantee Fund Trust for Micro & Small Enterprises (CGTMSE).

<table>
<tr><td rowspan="2">Objective: To make available collateral free credit facility to new and existing Micro & Small businesses subject to a limit of Rs 100 lakh per unit.</td><td>Performance during 2015-16 (up to 31/12/2015): 350056 applications approved with guarantee coverage of Rs 14,673 crore.</td></tr>
<tr><td>Performance since inception: 2160975 applications approved with coverage of Rs 103,864 crore.</td></tr>
</table>

Export Promotion of Capital Goods (EPCG).

<table>
<tr><td rowspan="2">Objective: To allow import of capital goods on zero duty subject to meeting export obligations.</td><td>Performance during 2015-16: Number of authorisations 22544 with FOB value of Rs 78,860 crore and duty savings of Rs 12619 crore.</td></tr>
<tr><td>Performance during 2016-17 (up to October 2016): Number of authorisations 13,585 with FOB value of Rs 50,359 crore and duty savings of Rs 8,668 crore.</td></tr>
</table>

Credit Linked Capital Subsidy Scheme (CLCSS).

<table>
<tr><td rowspan="2">Objective: To facilitate technology up-gradation. To enable beneficiary enterprises to avail institutional credit towards the purchase of machinery and technologies.</td><td>Performance during 2015-16 (up to 31/12/2015): 3,142 benefited units with an expenditure of Rs 203.76 crore.</td></tr>
<tr><td>Performance since inception: 22,380 benefited units with an expenditure of Rs 1349.63 crore.</td></tr>
</table>

Marketing Development Assistance (MDA) Scheme.

<table>
<tr><td rowspan="2">Objective: To help & encourage SMEs to tap & develop overseas market.</td><td>Performance during 2015-16 (up to 31/12/2015): Units participated–233. Expenditure–Rs 4.77 crore.</td></tr>
<tr><td>Performance since inception: Units participated–1476. Expenditure–Rs 28.76 crore.</td></tr>
</table>

Intellectual Property Rights

<table>
<tr><td rowspan="2">Objective: To enhance competitiveness through increased awareness of IPR.</td><td>Performance during 2015-16 (up to 31/12/2015): Awareness programmes held–26, Workshops–5, and IPR Facilitation Centres–3. Expenditure–Rs 1.73 crore.</td></tr>
<tr><td>Performance since inception: Awareness programmes held–308, Workshops–95, and IPR Facilitation Centres–31. Expenditure–Rs 13.69 crore.</td></tr>
</table>

12 INITIATIVES TAKEN BY GOVT OF INDIA FOR MSME SECTOR (2018) ANNOUNCED BY THE PRIME MINISTER

1. Loans up to Rs 1 crore within 59 minutes through online portal
2. Interest subvention of 2% for all GST registered MSMEs on fresh or incremental loans
3. All companies with a turnover more than Rs 500 crore must now compulsorily be brought on the Trade Receivables e-Discounting System (TReDS)
4. Public sector companies have now been asked to compulsorily procure 25%, instead of 20%, of their total purchases from MSMEs
5. Out of the 25% procurement mandated from MSMEs, 3% must now be reserved for women entrepreneurs
6. All public sector undertakings of the Union Government must now compulsorily be a part of Government e-Marketplace (GeM). They should also get all their vendors registered on GeM
7. Twenty hubs and 100 spokes in the form of tool rooms will be established across the country to facilitate product design
8. Clusters of pharma MSMEs will be formed and 70% cost of establishing these clusters will be borne by the Union Government
9. In order to simplify government procedures, the return under 8 labour laws and 10 Union regulations must now be filed only once a year
10. The establishments to be visited by an Inspector will be decided through a computerised random allotment
11. Environmental Clearance under air pollution and water pollution laws has been merged into one. Also, the return will be accepted through self-certification
12. For minor violations under the Companies Act, the entrepreneur will no longer have to approach the Courts, but can correct them through simple procedures

DISTRICT INDUSTRIES CENTRES

These have come up with the support of the Union Government in 1980s and the credit should go to late George Fernandes, the then Industries Minister.

Knowledge Hub

DICs should serve as Data and Information Centres. They should be effective windows of service to the emerging and existing enterprises. They should typically, therefore, have all wherewithal to acquire and disseminate knowledge.

Functionality

All the DICs should be having welcoming environment for the enterprises. They should have the shelf of schemes/projects with information on latest technologies relating to such schemes – availability, prices and delivery mechanisms. They should also have the e-library. The Schemes should be displayed with access points and incentives available either on an electronic mode or printed booklet both in the vernacular language and English.

IPOs as extension officers should have regular interaction with Banks and Business Development Service providers (Industries' Associations/ Federations) both in structured and informal manner.

Since all the Districts would be having building complexes of citizen interface at one single place, it is better that the DICs have a design that welcomes the industries.

Staff Reorientation

Change Management Programmes with focus on promoting industries should be held for all the staff of the DIC with each such programme not exceeding three days and each such programme having all the Assistant Directors and above from the Office of the Commissioner of Industries attending in order that all the officers would be on the same page in terms of performance of the envisioned objectives and goals of the DICs. Each such Change Management Programme should be with external support – like ASCI or EDI. The identified institution should be asked to make a presentation to the Committee consisting of Principal Secretary, CoI, and an external expert and design the Programme on the basis of recommendations of the Committee. Such three-day programmes should have a follow-up of one-day retreat after one month to monitor the assimilation process.

Performance appraisals of the officers and staff should be modified thereafter that should be related to the number of manufacturing enterprises, cluster development, health of the enterprises and industry feedback.

Relief to MSME Sector

The key sops include reduction of corporate tax from 30 per cent to 25 per cent for entities with a turnover of up to Rs 250 crore which was hitherto available up to Rs 50 crore. Import duties on some of the electronics and other items have been raised by 5 to 10 per cent to create domestic demand. The RBI provided a respite to GST-registered units by granting 90 days more time to repay loans of up to Rs 25 crore. All advances become NPAs in 90 days whereas MSME loans will now turn NPAs only after 180 days. GST information structure accommodates exemptions to enterprises with Rs 40 lakh turnover to be fully exempt; those up to Rs 1.5 crore turnover are placed in the Composition scheme where the enterprise has to submit quarterly and annual returns.

While Public Policy in India has accorded high priority to this sector in order to achieve balanced, sustainable, more equitable and inclusive growth in the country, credit markets have not moved closer to the MSMEs. Most banks opened up their schemes only to the small and medium enterprises with their larger exposure in the medium enterprises whose ability to provide strong collaterals are high. In other words, banks have only their marginal presence in the sector in spite of the policy thrust and incentive structure specific to micro enterprises. A policy correction seems necessary.

Policy risk or sovereign risk haunts the MSME sector even as several well-meaning policies have been formulated. For example, there exists a gap in perception of the lenders and MSME borrowers towards availability of finance. While the lenders felt that credit to the sector is expanding, the MSME borrowers felt that the lenders are not doing enough for the MSMEs and are catering more to the needs of the large corporate and medium enterprises.

Government e-Market Place (GeM)

The National Mission on Government e-Marketplace (GeM) was launched from 6 September to 17 October 2018, to accelerate the adoption of GeM and its use by major Central ministries, states and their agencies (including states, CPSUs/PSUs, local bodies). While promoting such adoption, the aim was to realise targets that

1. Promote inclusiveness;
2. Highlight transparency and efficiency in public procurement;
3. Achieve cashless, contactless and paperless transaction;
4. Lead to significant cost saving; and
5. Maximise ease in availability of all types of products & services.

Once the firms embrace technology and adapt openness in trade, this instrument would reduce the delays in realisation of the bills drawn on their buyers.

GeM is the National Public Procurement Portal and is an end-to-end, one-stop online marketplace for Central and state government ministries/departments, Central and State Public Sector Undertakings (CPSUs and SPSUs), autonomous institutions and local bodies, for procurement of common use goods and services.

In its less than two years of existence, as per the website of the MoMSME, GeM has nearly 5 lakh products available for online purchase with over 28,100 government organisations (Central and state governments and PSUs) registered and 144,554 sellers and service providers. GeM crossed 8.18 lakh transactions worth over Rs 12,440 crore as on 29 September 2018, with an average overall savings of 25 per cent. The Ministry of MSME launched a *delayed payment monitoring portal* (MSME SAMADHAAN) (http://samadhaan.msme.gov.in) in October 2017 which provides information about individual CPSEs/ Central ministries, state government, etc. regarding the payment pending with them in respect of the Micro & Small Enterprises (MSEs). The portal also empowers the MSEs to file their delayed payments related complaints online.

Several *Initiatives on the financial infrastructure side* have also been taken – including, among others – (i) Trade Receivables Discounting System (TReDS) — a digital platform where MSMEs can get access to credit by auctioning their trade receivables; (ii) Udyamimitra Platform: Virtual market place to provide 'End to End' solutions not only for credit delivery but also for the host of credit-plus services by way of hand-holding support, application tracking, multiple interface with stakeholders; (iii) CERSAI, in active coordination with Government of India and Reserve Bank has proposed setting up the movable asset registry; and (iv) Creation of a new category of lenders: Small Finance Banks, MUDRA Bank, Fintech Lenders.

Multi-stakeholder programmes

- *Make in India (2014)*. The initiative is designed to encourage investment, foster innovation, enhance skill development, protect intellectual property, and build best-in-class manufacturing infrastructure.
- *Startup India (2016)* was introduced as a flagship initiative of the government with the aim of building a strong eco-system for nurturing innovation and startups in the country.
- A version of Startup India was also launched for rural India, *Deen Dayal Upadhyay Swaniyojan Yojana*. The scheme provides basic skill sets for self-employment in various fields and also offers credit facilities and incubation centres wherever needed.

LOSING ON GAS

Jay LPG Bottling Plant Ltd.

M/s Jay LPG Bottling Plant (P) Ltd. was set up by Prasad, an engineer and a postgraduate in Business Management. It is a closely-held family enterprise. During 1998, the promoter, enthused by the government policy allowing private entrepreneurs to enter into an area where demand existed, viz., supply of gas to households in convenient packs, set up the unit with technology put on a turnkey basis. Both the Chairman and the Managing Director had considerable experience in the management and technology aspects. The unit has, however, failed to achieve break-even right from inception.

The firm had put in an equity of Rs 93.50 lakh and took a term loan from the Central Bank of India to the tune of Rs 125 lakh. Its working capital limits are to the extent of Rs 31 lakh.

The unit has suffered operating losses during the years 1999-2003, although on a reducing scale during the years 2001-03. The bank has rescheduled the term loan – taking one year for its decision during which period the interest accumulations eroded the advantage of such reschedulement.

This is a unit where adverse government policies like crowding the sector with too many private entrepreneurs and also allowing external brands like Coca Cola, Pepsi were responsible for the failure.

7

Business Development Service Providers

Introduction

So far, we have noticed the following advantages of Small and Medium-sized Enterprises (SMEs):

- SMEs can create wealth;
- SMEs can provide employment;
- They have a greater proclivity to innovate than their larger counterparts and, therefore, play an important role in the country responding to a myriad of changes in economic, technological and social environment;
- SMEs can make an important contribution to the infrastructure needed to support larger competitive business;
- They can help to counter regional economic decline because SMEs could survive in limited markets while their elder brothers cannot;
- Other benefits include increased competition, choice and diversity, regionalisation of sectors, political stability and social cohesion;

- ❖ Their frailty lies in information asymmetry; inadequate capacities to cope with changes quickly; unwillingness to share and compete in markets.

Each enterprise may have its own strengths. But there will be issues that need resolution only through collectivism and cooperation. Somehow, over the years, while such collective entities in the name of Associations and Federations sprang up both in terms of the sectors and otherwise, they have forsaken their representative status and the vibrant category close to the large enterprises have started representing the issues of the sector or lobbying for the sector – CII, FICCI, PHDFC to mention a few. It is not unlikely that some real issues of MSMEs get crowded out in the process.

Certain regions have represented remarkable strength in the SME sector, and they have built good lobbying and representative status: to name a few of them: FISME (Delhi and Northern Region), TANSTIA, CODISSIA, KASSIA, ALEAP etc. Similarly, product associations/ federations like the pharma, plastics, automotive components, textiles etc., created a good negotiation platform through a variety of interventions that included mentoring, training, and IPR protection.

SMEs face discriminatory barriers that prevent a level playing field and these are generally classified as 'market failures'. Market failure is generally referred in the context of perfect markets and one must be aware that markets are never perfect. Interventions in perfect markets do not result in improvements in markets. The value of any apparent benefits in one area would be outweighed by the cost of displacement effects elsewhere, and there would be no net economic benefit. However, after a disruption in the market there may be some factors that delay the market to return to perfection. Such factors are referred to as 'market failure'. Interventions to address these inherently temporary factors could produce benefits. These interventions would be external and would be addressed by a service provider. Traditional market failure arguments in the case of SMEs usually concern problems related to information asymmetry, economies of scale, and imperfect appropriation of returns. Smaller firms generally have fewer financial, human and technical resources, which constrain their ability to take advantage of given opportunities, particularly those associated with economies of scale. Small enterprises also suffer more from information gaps and have difficulty evaluating the benefits of, for instance, adopting new technologies or entering distant markets. We have seen in the previous chapter the problems of the SMEs accessing finance from the banks and capital markets either due to a lack of collateral, unproven track record and risk-adverse investors; at the same time, they lack information on alternative sources. SMEs do not have the ability to fight out legal issues both due to high costs and ignorance of right legal advice. They do not have the ability to withstand for long time the pressures in case they encounter legal problems.

Regulatory Aspects

Insufficient coordination between different government bodies and policies has reduced the efficiency of SME policies and thus limited their potential to fuel economic growth. The Micro, Small and Medium Enterprise Development Act 2006, a rule bound legislation has evolved over the last decade into a facilitating Act. The state governments have their own views and rationale in promoting SME activities specific to their state economies. Attention seems to be on giving cumulative effects of the regulations ensuring growth of SMEs.

Systemic Failures

There has been insufficient attention accorded to SMEs in the broader economic context, reflecting an outdated perception that these enterprises are of little importance to technology development or growth despite their potential for employment generation. Systemic failures also exist on a global scale as national policies regarding SMEs sometimes contradict and cancel each other. National policy measures may lead to unintended impacts on smaller firms in other smaller countries. Various factors may interact to cause discrimination against new comers such as registration procedures, norms and standards, labour and product market regulations, and so on which are particularly disadvantageous to SMEs trying to access global markets. Lack of inter-state coordination to facilitate cross-border SMEs to grow is another failure that would need to be tackled.

Table : A View of Market Imperfections, their causes and remedies

Market Gap	Causes	Remedies
Supply factors: Entrepreneurs	Social and economic bias in favour of employment instead of enterprise promotion	*Social security system Education Fiscal system
Innovations	Inadequate R&D	Research Policy; R&D expenditure; Improving collaboration and coordination between the SMEs and R&D institutions; Fiscal incentives
Lack of Capital	Financial exclusion; Distortions in capital markets	Competition policy; Supportive lending policies; credit guarantees; monitoring the targets carefully
Labour	Imperfections in labour markets	Social security system; social environment; Housing policy; Training and Education; Labour relations policy; Minimum wages policy
Lack of or Inadequate premises	Imperfections in property markets	Urban development; planning regulations like zoning; environment protection; and investment in infrastructure

Market Gap	Causes	Remedies
Regulatory Compliance	Bureaucratic approach to issues; growth of and change in governments; federal set up	Simplification; Separate law with transparent rules; exemptions; changes in local taxation laws; Reorganisation of state and Central government set-up; Single window clearances within set time frame
Market	Supplier markets and seller markets are imperfect	Competition policy; government 'crowding out'; market promotion and development

MSMEs, if they were to develop, require access to a range of skills and abilities in areas such as organisation, management, production, marketing, selling, strategy, finance and law. They know that they need them but do not seek them. Some of the explanations offered for their reluctance are:

- Owner entrepreneurs fear that exposing their strategies to others may lead to their ideas being stolen by others;
- There is a reluctance to approach experts because of their fear that experts despise their efforts due to their poor interpersonal and technical skills to deal with their sophisticated consultants;
- They lack information on availability and cost of such services to make a rational choice;
- They feel that the available support is not appropriate to their needs;
- They might be discouraged by the price of advice;
- The content of support would appear 'top-down' instead of 'participative'.

Many factors create an enterprise culture and the values, beliefs and assumptions that are widely shared by members of a community will not be the same in India, Pakistan, Bangladesh, the US and Europe and East Asia. Bringing about coordination between government, media and popular opinion supportive of entrepreneurship is a task that is best done by experts in Business Development Services (BDS) set-up.

There is also a need to distinguish between general education and specific education to build entrepreneurial skills. The educational system can be used for:

- Creating an awareness of the role of entrepreneurs in the economy;
- Encouraging commercial awareness;
- Raising the social standing of the entrepreneur;
- Creating an awareness of entrepreneurship as a career option;
- Developing the necessary entrepreneurial skills;
- Stimulating the application of entrepreneurial knowledge and qualities.

Several Universities and Management Education Institutions in India have started Enterprise Development Departments and Incubation cells in India. These are set to grow phenomenally over the next few years, thanks to the latest thrust given by the MSME department.

If we want MSMEs to make significant contribution to the economy, then it makes sense to assist these enterprises that are basically viable until their expertise and experience improve and allow them to reap the benefits. BDS providers offer such facilitation through hand-holding for the start-ups, advice during the growth process and help with coping strategies in competitive environment that may sometimes lead to franchising, acquisitions, joint ventures, and mergers both domestically and globally. They guide the entrepreneurs in seeking proper legal advice at the right time. They help in preparing business plans and periodical review to achieve business targets.

These providers are in the shape of mentors, advisors, consultants, technical experts, legal experts at the individual level; a group of them at the non-government level; industry associations and their special windows of assistance (CODISSIA, Coimbatore; TANSTIA-FNF Centre, Chennai; FISME, New Delhi; COSIA, Thane, Maharashtra etc.)

Roles and Responsibilities of BDS Providers

In India, most BDS facilitators and BDS providers are in formative stages and only a few are close to maturing. Therefore, while developing the content of this chapter, European models are taken into consideration.

Start-ups and existing enterprises are supported by trained BDS facilitators and BDS providers in a six-month time period. The demand-driven six-month BDS cycle approach is a participatory method comprising of situation and problem analysis and action planning (one month) and the implementation of services to overcome the identified constraints (five months). The facilitators work with entrepreneurs during this six-month period and help the latter with refining their proposals to set up enterprises simultaneously complying with regulatory rigour. Usually they work in clusters of 10-15 enterprises. The Situation Analysis contains the following issues:

Name/ Activity Place/ Equipment	Products/ services	Supply/ sales Clients/ Marketing	Personnel/ Business Management	Costs per month	Problems identified by the entrepreneur himself/ herself and his/her proposals for solutions
Enterprise -1					
Enterprise - 2					

The facilitator documents the 10-15 entrepreneurs' problems and solutions and designs an action plan that contains the problems identified, self-help initiative to solve the problems and additional support required from the BDS provider.

Types of Support

Depending on the needs, market research, product development, business planning, accounting, and cost calculation, access to finance, government subsidies and procedures to access them; support for administrative problems, tax issues, premises, trade fair participation, export-import procedures, linkage to technology promotion and development, organisational development and linkage to industry associations or chambers would be in the framework of supports. The main task of BDS facilitator is not to solve the problems/constraints by himself but to link to competent professional BDS providers, such as training establishments, marketing specialists, chartered accountants, cost accountants, legal experts, trade fair organisers and Industry and Trade Chambers. Those who are found to be having trouble in resolving the identified issues after six months will be hand-held unless the issues rest on non-resolvable fundamentals of business. In the latter case, the BDS facilitator moves to other groups of enterprises. There will be follow-up and supervision. The supervisor is known as BDS Team Leader. At the end of the six-month period the BDS facilitators write a simple report on what they have achieved:

Name of Business	Support Activities identified	Support Activities Achieved	Impact and Remarks
Enterprise – 1			
Enterprise – 2			

BDS is used in value chain development in order to solve important problems. Linkage is the main task of BDS facilitators, even if minor problems can be solved by themselves. BDS is used in industrial cluster development, in sector specific and gender specific interventions and as follow-up system for start-ups after initial entrepreneurial training.

Networking is their key function. [This has been proved in successful **evaluations done by GTZ in Mali, 1998, (Gerhard Ebert)** and Ethiopia 2005 (Chris Reichert, Sonja Kurz)]. For further reference, the reader is advised to browse through www.bds-forum.net with all strategies, tool kits, newsletters, etc.

Any Association serving as BDS provider would need a strong financial support and this would come only when the members regularly support with subscriptions and periodically with investments in BDS activities. This would require sacrificing the time of office-bearers more than others. Hence rotation of office-bearers annually would render equity of contribution from the members.

Governance plays a crucial role. The Association should function under well accepted governance systems. The Boards must have half-yearly and annual retreats for proper introspection and document the required corrective mechanisms.

The management of Associations must be thinly staffed and well networked. Networking is the name of the game for effective communication both within the Association and outside. The Associations should have affiliations with academic and research institutions with periodical evaluation as to the outcomes. Members should feel and express the benefits accruing from such collaborations and affiliations. The member services could include travel and tourism, holding frequent vendor management exchanges, sub-contract exchanges, etc.

The strength of BDS will, therefore, depend upon the extent they are able to serve their members both in and outside the domain.

8

Access to Finance

Most MSMEs in India face poor access to finance within a financial system dominated by banks. The following points will conclusively highlight the scale of funding challenges faced by the Indian MSME Sector.

As per IFC, the total financing demand of the Indian MSME sector is around Rs 32.5 trillion – comprised of entrepreneur's contribution of Rs 4.6 trillion and estimated external finance demand of Rs 27.9 trillion.

Considering that the MSMEs have access to formal finance of around Rs 10 trillion, the sector is grappling with a formal credit gap of around Rs 17.9 trillion. The enormity of the financial challenge is clear from the fact that the credit gap is close to twice the actual outstanding amount of formal credit extended to the sector.

The Prime Minister's Task Force on Micro, Small and Medium Enterprises (MSMEs) recommended that the government should ensure strict adherence to stipulated targets by the commercial banks for the micro enterprises (viz. 20 per cent year-on-year growth for micro and small enterprises lending with 60 percent apportionment for manufacturing micro sector) that is particularly important in this context. However, no more than 16 per cent year-over-year (YOY) growth is seen anywhere.

Several measures have been taken by RBI to improve credit flow to MSMEs. For instance, a Standing Advisory Committee on SSI Credit monitors the flow of credit on a quarterly basis. Regular guidelines are issued to the banks for promoting credit to small enterprises. These guidelines on lending to the priority sector have been revised by the RBI from time to time. The latest revision of guidelines was in 2011 following the recommendations of the Working Group set up by the RBI with M.V. Nair as Chairman.

Credit delivery at the state level takes place through the following institutions:

- The State Financial Corporations (SFCs) which provide term loans to small and medium enterprises.
- The State Small Industries Export Corporations which procure and distribute scarce raw material, machinery on hire purchase, assist in marketing, quality support, etc.
- The State Industrial Development Corporations which acquire land and offer plots and sheds to entrepreneurs.
- State Trading Corporations which assist in exports, provide market intelligence at national and international levels and operate showrooms.
- A few states have regional development corporations for individual regions.
- A few states have set up venture capital funds.
- A few states have set up Institutes for Entrepreneurship development.

However, only a few of the institutions have remained active in the recent past and are fulfilling the needs of the SME segment to their full potential. For example, out of 18 SFCs in the country, only four SFCs and a twin-function IDC are active in lending to the SME segment. Most of the SFCs have faced financial problems due to the way they are structured, high interference from the state government, inadequate capitalisation or lack of sufficient capital infusion from time to time, high NPA percentage level, etc.

In this regard, the various initiatives taken by the Government of India and Reserve Bank such as adoption of the Business Correspondent (BC) model, relaxation of KYC norms, simplified branch authorisation, preparation of board approved financial inclusion plans, mandatory opening of 25 per cent of new branches in unbanked rural centres, preparation of financial inclusion plans by banks, etc. are expected to accelerate the process of financial inclusion in the country and the MSME sector is expected to be among the beneficiaries of the same through better access to bank credit.

The M.V. Nair Committee Report brings to light some of the inside stories of expansion of credit to micro enterprises over the years. The Report clearly points out that financing by banks under the MSE category remains stagnant; progress has been largely in terms of percentage share of credit outflow, and not in terms of number of accounts. The Committee, therefore, has recommended a minimum annual growth rate of 15 per cent in the number of accounts every year. The flow of credit to the MSME sector in India is, indeed, the sum total of some objective and subjective factors. The effects of these two sets of factors get reflected at any particular point.

A number of cross-country studies and country case studies show that MSMEs face considerable financing constraints, which hamper their growth in terms of profits and turnover. Asymmetric information between the lender and the borrower of firms may hamper the readiness of lenders to provide finance, which, in turn, would hamper the growth performance of the borrowers. Studies find that more cash flow fosters growth, reiterating the impact of financing constraints on growth. The probability of financial obstacles (proxy by age, size and other firm features) is, generally, found to affect growth.

The literature on gaps and market failures demonstrate that, irrespective of new financial products in the MSME sector, such a gap is prevalent. It exists in the market for commercial loans, no-bank depth financing, mezzanine financing, informal capital, institutional venture capital, and market for IPOs. Suppliers of capital, both lenders and investors, have decried a gap in the form of a shortage of investible opportunities and bankable SMEs.[1] The comparative experience of various countries indicates a threat-credit crunch. While the nature and magnitude are different, this problem plagues most countries of the world. The problem of access to finance for the MSME sector is intrinsically linked to the problem of financial exclusion in the country. The ability of banks to rapidly increase their coverage of MSMEs through credit facilities would depend on their ability to expand their reach to the hitherto unbanked segments of the country.

Challenges in Delivering MSME Credit through Banks

Despite the efforts of GoI and RBI, banks remain somewhat disengaged in the process of increasing access of credit to MSMEs and the attitude of bankers towards MSME remains a major roadblock. Since SSI credit is part of priority sector credit and banking regulations specify targets in terms of meeting priority sector credit, banks take the easy way out of meeting priority sector targets through the Rural Infrastructure Development Fund (RIDF).

While, according to the Fourth All India Census of MSMEs, 93.5 per cent of the enterprises belong to the bottom of the pyramid, and are micro in nature, impact can best be measured in terms of the number of units that are addressed by priority sector credit, rather than the volume of credit that goes to the micro enterprises.

Loans not exceeding Rs 50,000 per head, extended directly by banks to poorer sections of society, and through the mechanism of self-help groups, are classified as micro credit, which again falls under the priority sector. According to the latest figures, micro credit constitutes 0.7 per cent of the priority sector portfolio of public sector banks and 3.67 per cent in the case of private sector banks. It is also important to note that micro credit and micro finance have gained substantial importance at the global level as also in India.

Attitudinal Disposition of Lenders

Most financing institutions view MSMEs as high risk enterprises. This is basically a question of attitudes towards enterprise development than the associated risks. There are a few important attributes for being a good credit analyst: knowledge of the entrepreneur; knowledge of the enterprise and knowledge of the environment (the three 'E's). Knowledge of the entrepreneur can take place by following the KYC (Know Your Customer) norms and due diligence enquiries from the market place. Knowledge of the enterprise and environment requires investment and time on the part of the credit analyst. Since the sector manufactures more than 6000 products, it would be difficult for the banks' credit analyst to have knowledge about the activity to which he proposes to lend and the regulations surrounding the product that the enterprise is engaged in. Unfortunately, the lender in possession of the key resource, money, refuses to see merit in such investment in knowledge acquisition and also does not accept that he does not have the knowledge. He assumes supremacy over the entrepreneur and tries to dictate the gestation periods, investment margins and often also the cash flows of some products that are governed by seasonality of either inputs or outputs or both.

Ever since the formation of credit committees, banks at the state and sub-state levels for sanction of advances for the SME sector are used to making assessments more by the balance sheet than by the credentials of the entrepreneur or prospects of success of the enterprise. SME proposals are sponsored by the branches at the instance of the marketing personnel; the bank branches enquire into the credentials if any queries are raised by the credit committees. In this process the biggest casualty is the process of due diligence. Due to acute shortage of field executives, on-site supervision has become a rarity. There are only a few exceptions to this situation. The whole process has led to overconfidence on the part of both the banks and entrepreneurs leading eventually to creating more NPAs.

Risk-sharing facilities coupled with the introduction of best practice SME lending approaches are the key interventions that can help banks provide credit to SMEs. These interventions need to accompany enhancements to the enabling environment for SME lending such as credit bureaus, collaterals and insolvency regimes.

All the Associations of MSMEs that represented to the High-Level Committee (2018) of the RBI mentioned 'access to timely and adequate credit for the MSMEs' as an issue that requires comprehensive and out-of-the box solutions.

The issue assumes significance from the following angles:

1. The Micro and Small Enterprise sector contributed to a robust job growth of 3.25 per cent per annum during 2014-18. But the Banks' reluctance to revive the potentially viable enterprises has created fear of loss of jobs – particularly, the skilled due to forced closure of MSMEs.
2. Manufacturing growth is not that robust as growth of services sector.
3. Lending to MSMEs has been on the decline during the last two years, notwithstanding the drive for Make-in-India, Start-up India, Stand-up India and the launching of a major initiative through MUDRA, TReDS, GeMs, etc.
4. Several lending institutions have been showing up excesses in recovery of loans for the MSME sector compared to the other sectors, in a collateralised lending regime.

This chapter therefore examines the supply-side and demand-side constraints to credit growth, efficiency of credit delivery instruments, RBI regulations, the roles of public sector banks, private sector banks, SFCs, NBFCs, MFIs, SIDBI's support system, insurance and guarantee mechanisms, restructuring and revival of the failed enterprises, exit route for the disappointed or failed enterprises, and suggests remedial measures.

Credit Products and Issues

1 • Investment Credit; Working Capital/Overdraft/Liquidity

2 • Loans & Borrowings for Expansion, Renovation, Diversification, Revival and Rehabilitation

3 • Role of Financial Agencies, Government Schemes

4 • Credit Rating, Business Risks, Credit Delivery, Exit of MSEs in Distress

Working Capital for Micro and Small Enterprises

Inadequacies and untimely roll outs of working capital have been the major problems of Micro and Small Enterprises that are mostly dependent on debt for their survival and growth. Several Committees have articulated this problem that has endemic proportions. As many as 95 per cent of the units are proprietor managed whose time for borrowing money should not take more than 2 to 3 per cent of the management time otherwise the cost of borrowing will be onerous. The effort of credit reform should be to minimise this effort.

Existing Guidelines

1. Banks are mandated to calculate the working capital at a minimum 20 per cent of the projected turnover following the Nayak Committee recommendations (1991). The threshold limit has been enhanced to Rs 5 crore (2018).
2. Up to Rs 25 lakh of working capital and investment credit have to be extended to Micro enterprises as composite loan without collateral security.
3. Collateral-free lending has been extended for manufacturing MSMEs up to Rs 200 lakh.

Banks like SBI have set up Small Medium Enterprises City Credit Centres (SME CCC) and all loans up to Rs 50 lakh need to be sanctioned by the centre and not at the branch level. When the mandates 1 to 3 exist, there is need for empowering all the branch managers to sanction under these stipulations. It is only those that cross the threshold that should come for higher level of administration for sanction. While the RBI has been periodically holding one-day workshops aimed at capacity building, its emphasis on and monitoring of the above guidelines need much to be desired.

Work Order-based Lending

All branches should be mandated to provide working capital on cash flow basis and not on Balance Sheet Ratios. Further, when the unit produces a work order that crosses the existing working capital limits, the branch managers should be empowered to sanction up to 75 per cent of the work order even if the original sanctioned limits are overstepped and the branches need to report for control to the concerned authorities online for review and approval that should not exceed 24 hours of the request for such limit. Branch managers should do their regular due diligence of such requests.

Some banks have excellent working capital products like SMEplus but their reach is minimal due to banks extending them only on the basis of availability of collateral adequacy.

Banks extend such facilities more to the Service sector enterprises than to manufacturing enterprises. These excesses can be minimised through an effective monitoring mechanism. Since all the banks are computerised, it should be easier to call for disaggregated data on different parameters with checks and cross-checks.

Supervised lending has become a rarity due to acute shortage of field staff although charges for unit inspections are invariably levied on the units. There are unscrupulous borrowers who need to be proceeded against at the first sign of deviation from the stipulations of sanction. This will distance willful defaulter right at the inception stage. Overvalued stocks and expired stocks getting into stock statements can be avoided only with at least quarterly surprise inspections by the managers/field officers. There are no short cuts to arresting deviant behavior.

Micro and Small Enterprise Facilitation Council (MSEFC)

Most micro and small enterprises suffer from delayed payments for their supplies and services. Several contractual engagements with both the government and public sector undertakings also are not honoured.

In line with the long-standing demand of the small-scale sector to alleviate the problem of delayed payments, the Delayed Payments Act came into being in 1993. The hope that the small-scale industries would be relieved of the stress in working capital was short-lived due to ineffective implementation. The Act was amended in September 1998 to provide for payment of penal interest at 150 per cent of the prime lending rate of SBI, defining default period as 120 days. It also provided for an alternative mechanism of arbitration and conciliation and also redefined the term supplier to include any institution, agency or undertaking notified as such by the Union Government. Industrial Facilitation Councils empowered to act as arbitrators/conciliators were to be notified by the state/UT governments. The amendments were effected to strengthen the Act, to make it more useful without disturbing the buyer–seller cordial relations and to provide relief to the small suppliers from undergoing the cumbersome recourse of legal redressal through civil suits.

Subsequently, in 2006 when the MSME Development Act was brought in, the Delayed Payments Act was subsumed in Sections 15 to 18 of the MSMED Act whereby the MSE Facilitation Councils replaced the Industrial Facilitation Councils. The well-intentioned provisions, however, are still not delivering the intended reliefs.

Jurisdiction: Section 18(4)

1. Several MSEs enter into sale contracts and PPPs that specify the jurisdiction of the dispute within the respective state. Unless the MSMED Act has a provision to overrule such jurisdiction, the claim order will be embroiled in a legal tangle involving huge legal expense and leading to further delay in realising the claim from the respondent.
2. Most such disputes are formidable when the respondent is either a government department or public sector undertaking.
3. It is incumbent on the payee to remit 75 per cent of the claim amount in case the Council's order is contested in the High Court. But such remittance being made into the Court and not into the account of the firm, the sword of NPA still hangs on the neck of the enterprise. It is a matter for consideration whether the related High Court in such dispute could straight away inform the Bank where the firm holds its accounts that the Deposit is held by the Court in its name so that the proceedings of the Bank due to declaring the Account as NPA and further proceedings under SARFAESI (Securitisation and Reconstruction

of Financial Assets and Enforcement of Securities Interest) Act can be halted and the unit allowed to carry on its normal production activity with renewal of their credit limits.

4. Clause 4 of Section 18 has overriding clause that is not honoured by most state governments and the High Courts as well. Therefore, strengthening this provision is extremely important when the disputed claim gets remittance of 75 per cent into the Court upfront.

There is, therefore, imminent need for amending the MSMED Act 2006 suitably and the revised Policy for the sector should include this aspect.

1. *The Council is expected to deliver the judgment within 90 days of lodging of the claim. Not infrequently, this time lag expands at the Council itself due to administrative reasons as the Chairman is obliged to perform other statutory functions as Director of Industries within the ordained timelines of the state government.*
2. *Ninety days' delay, if unresolved in terms of actual realisation of the supply bill, turns the account into NPA. Ninety days was fixed when the NPA norm was 120 days' overdue position. Therefore, this 90 days' timeline has to be reduced to 60 days and that too mandatorily.*
3. *The Council that meets once in a month should meet at fortnightly intervals to provide reasonable scope for hearing both sides providing for either party unable to present itself when called upon to do so by the Council for any justifiable reason. No more than two adjournments shall be allowed in such cases by the Chairman. It is desirable that this is provided in the statute itself instead of rules.*
4. *After the Council adjudicates on the claim, if the respondent does not honour the order, the firm has to file an Execution Petition within the respective jurisdiction after waiting for three months from the date of the order and this is governed by the CPC. Therefore, the intended settlement does not take place.*

Hence it is important that the issue of the jurisdiction should have an over-riding provision over any and all other such clauses in any agreement between the disputant parties. All said and done, the small enterprises being captive suppliers do not have the muscle to alter the PPP clauses even when some of them contravene law.

Chairman

- Chairman of the Council being a quasi-judiciary function shall be no less than Director of the Industries. This is imperative for the other reason that the Director acting as Chairman has full knowledge of (a) the functioning of the inter-relationship between the buyer and seller as a contractual arrangement; (b) the functioning of the industry itself from the date of registration to its demonstrated ability of reaching production capacity and standards of supply of goods and services by it; and (c) of the transactional milieu of the industries with the Banks and FIs, as Chairman of SLIIC Sub-committee.
- This position shall get the acceptance from all the state governments several state governments, notwithstanding the existence of such Councils in their own state, refuse to honour the verdict of the Council.

Training

The Chairman and the Members of the Council shall be given a five-day training in the essential laws that govern the contracts, sale of goods Act, taxation laws and the jurisdictional issues, Arbitration and Conciliation Act 1996 and its further amendments through Case Laws in the State Judicial Academy or the National Law University/School. This will enable them to come to quicker decisions on the disputes between the buyers and sellers and lessen the burden of arguments on either side which is necessary to judge the case within two or three hearings.

Whenever the Courts receive petitions relating to the debts due to the MSMEs from the government departments or PSUs, it is a matter of introspection as to the reasons for Judiciary at different tiers not asking them to specify what according to them meets with the contractual arrangement and pass the orders in just one or two hearings. This single step could settle many grievances relating to MSEs before they are declared NPAs by the Banks and FIs.

Structurally, this is inadequate and inappropriate intervention for delayed payments issue. Weakling MSEs drawing bills mostly on government entities, financed by government-owned banks expecting resolution at the Government set up arbitration mechanism have little to gain. The Award, where given, requires resolution at the field level. When contested, the Courts hardly insisted upon 75 per cent upfront payment of the contested amount. Even where the amount was parked with the Courts, it hardly proved a resolution as the Bank books continue to show it as NPA warranting SARFAESI Act proceedings. IBC is no reprieve.

The quasi-judiciary functionary heading the MSEFC should know how to deliver a speaking order. There were number of cases where the Courts have pointed out lapses in this regard. This requires knowledge and skills germane to the Act.

Role of Small Industries Development Bank of India

Small Industries Development Bank of India (SIDBI), set up in 1990, finances both refinance and direct finance. Its refinance is to the PLIs such as Banks, State Finance Corporations and other intermediaries like the MFIs and NBFCs who extend direct finance to the MSMEs as defined under the MSMED Act 2006. It claims particular focus on niche areas like risk capital/equity, sustainable finance for promoting energy efficiency and cleaner production, receivable financing, service sector financing, etc. Direct finance to MSMEs is extended through the Bank's network of 83 branch offices located all over the country.

In addition to its direct and indirect operations, SIDBI also plays a nodal agency role in implementation of various schemes for MSME sector undertaken by Government of India, viz. Credit Linked Capital Subsidy Scheme (CLCSS), Technology Upgradation Fund Scheme for Textiles Industry (TUFS), Integrated Development of Leather Sector Scheme (IDLSS), Scheme of Technology Upgradation/Setting up/

Modernisation/Expansion of Food Processing Industries (FPTUFS) and Technology and Quality Upgradation (TEQUP) Scheme to encourage MSMEs in adopting modern/energy efficient technologies.

While as many as 33 funds are floated both by NABARD and SIDBI for the MSME sector, we could not find any review as to the efficiency of operation of each of the funds from the point of view of either speed of delivery or the objectives assigned to each such fund. Both Venture Capital (SIDBI's and others), Angel funding have reached the real estate, micro finance, and ITES.

SIDBI has not provided the leadership it was expected to in lending to the small industries going by its performance thus far, which helped more collateral-based lending and medium enterprises rather than micro and small. It could devise new products based on equity as in the Small Business Administration, USA, for the micro and small enterprises and create or support handholding institutions through strategic partnerships. The Institution begs restructuring in the current phase of development of the nation.

Loan-size and Credit Flow

Irrespective of the life cycle of a firm, the focus of an MSME policy needs to address the relative deprivation of these enterprises. While the larger enterprises get a relative advantage in terms of the cost of credit, the smaller units have a relative disadvantage. It is in this context that new institutional structures and policies have come up in the past. For example, MUDRA is a major institutional platform. The Prime Minister's Jan Dhan Yojana is a new policy initiative. While Jan Dhan is more a savings-driven and financial inclusion-driven initiative, the loan product of Rs 5000 per such account holder made limited strides till MUDRA scheme was introduced.

Micro Units Development & Refinance Agency Scheme

MUDRA, which stands for Micro Units Development & Refinance Agency Ltd, is a financial institution set up by the Government of India for development and refinancing micro units' enterprises. It was announced by the Finance Minister while presenting the Union Budget for FY 2016-17. The purpose of MUDRA is to provide funding to the non-corporate small business sector through various Last Mile Financial Institutions like Banks, NBFCs and MFIs.

The biggest bottleneck to the growth of entrepreneurship in the Non–Corporate Small Business Sector (NCSB) is lack of financial support to this sector. More than 80 per cent of this sector does not have access to formal sources of finance. The Government of India is setting up MUDRA Bank through a statutory enactment for catering to the needs of the NCSB segment or the informal sector for bringing them in the mainstream. Pending enactment of an act for MUDRA Bank, a Non-Banking Finance Company as MUDRA Ltd has been set up as a subsidiary of SIDBI.

Under the aegis of Pradhan Mantri MUDRA Yojana (PMMY), MUDRA would be responsible for refinancing all Last Mile Financiers such as Non-Banking Finance Companies, Societies, Trusts, Section 8 Companies [formerly Section 25], Co-operative Societies, Small Banks, Scheduled Commercial Banks and Regional Rural Banks which are in the business of lending to micro/small business entities engaged in manufacturing, trading and services activities such as shopkeepers, fruits / vegetable vendors, truck operators, food-service units, repair shops, machine operators, small industries, artisans, food processors and others, in rural and urban areas. MUDRA would also partner with state/regional level financial intermediaries to provide finance to Last Mile Financier of small/micro business enterprises.

Loans are categorised into Shishu, Kishor and Tarun. These products have been designed to cater to customers operating at the lower end of the enterprise spectrum. These groups signify the stage of growth/ development and funding needs of the beneficiary micro unit/ entrepreneur and also to provide a reference point for the next phase of graduation/growth to look forward to. The financial limit for these schemes is :-

a) Shishu: covering loans up to Rs 50,000
b) Kishor: covering loans above Rs 50,000 and up to Rs 5 lakh
c) Tarun: covering loans above Rs 5 lakh and up to Rs 10 lakh

MUDRA's delivery channel is conceived to be through the route of refinance primarily to Banks/NBFCs/MFIs.

All loans sanctioned on or after 8 April 2015 up to a loan size of Rs 10 lakh for non-farm income generating activities will be branded as PMMY loans.

Any Indian Citizen who has a business plan for a non-farm income generating activity such as manufacturing, processing, trading or service sector whose credit need is less than Rs 10 lakh can approach either a Bank, MFI or NBFC for availing of MUDRA loans under PMMY. The usual terms and conditions of the lending agency may have to be followed for availing of loans under PMMY. The lending rates are as per the RBI guidelines issued in this regard from time to time.

There is no subsidy for the loan given under PMMY. However, if the loan proposal is linked to some Government scheme, wherein the Government is providing capital subsidy, it will be eligible under PMMY also.

MUDRA Card is an innovative credit product wherein the borrower can avail of credit in a hassle free and flexible manner. It will provide a facility of working capital arrangement in the form of CC/OD to the borrower. Since MUDRA Card will be RuPay's debit card, it can be used for drawing cash from ATM or Business Correspondent or make purchase using Point of Sale (POS) machine. Facility is also there to repay the amount, as and when, surplus cash is available, thereby reducing the interest cost.

MUDRA's role, as has been announced, includes:

- Policy formulation for financing micro enterprises, small business firms and registration of MFIs;
- Rating and accreditation of MFIs;
- Setting benchmarks for best practices of lending, client protection and customer service;
- Providing technology support to cover the last mile entity;
- Formulating and running a credit guarantee scheme for micro enterprises;
- Setting up a good architecture for micro finance; and

❖ Acting as a development and refinance institution.

It started off more as a refinancing institution. Banks that did not find human resources to lend for the micro and small enterprises and falling short of the RBI's priority sector allocation for the MSE manufacturing sector **added Rs 1.25 trillion** or 1.7 per cent of the total loan book under MUDRA scheme at the end of March 2016, according to data revealed by SIDBI. Out of 32.7 million borrowers, 30.3 million borrowers were in the Shishu category. MUDRA did not either do due diligence or monitoring of the accounts. Achievements under the MUDRA scheme have to be cautiously taken in the above context. But all these loans are guaranteed by the National Credit Guarantee Trust Ltd., set up by the Union government. Adverse selection is bound to hit these loans and eventually might spell disaster for the guarantee mechanism.

This is where the design and implementation of PMMY becomes critical. If the outcomes are all about the quantum of loans disbursed, it only reflects an entitlement. Some hard truths about economic value added in MSME and in large enterprises reveal that the monitoring mechanisms for loan disbursals under various categories of MUDRA need to be looked at from the livelihood enrichment with PMMY. In January 2019, RBI expressed concern over the MUDRA loans picking up NPAs of the order of Rs 11,000 crore, confirming the anxieties expressed by the author when the scheme was announced.

Financing by Non-Banking Finance Companies

In a traditional lending fort of SFCs and commercial banks, NBFCs made a swift entry. The process through which this shift is occurring can throw some lessons for the existing SFCs and banks as these NBFCs have lately become the favoured destinations of quite a few MSMEs.

Most NBFCs lend to SMEs and only a few select NBFCs to micro enterprises as they finance low risk, well secured through collateral enterprises with a ticket size of over Rs 50 lakh and under Rs 500 lakh. This is precisely what NBFCs such as Edelweiss, Indiabulls Housing, IndoStar Capital, Dewan Housing and IIFL Group, among others, are cashing in on as they remain optimistic about the funding scenario. On an average, they already report 25 per cent of their assets devoted to the small-scale sector. NBFCs normally lend in the secured category, thereby ensuring minimal defaults.

NBFCs like Fullerton India; Religare Finvest; Shriram City Union Finance; Bajaj Finserve; HDB (an NBFC promoted by HDFC); Capital First etc., concentrate on financing the micro and small enterprises as they will be amenable to counseling and mentoring better than the medium enterprises. They pool the micro loans for a particular activity or particular class of entrepreneurs that would allow them to save on procuring raw material in bulk and source the markets better. They choose a compact area or adopt a project approach so that the monitoring and supervision costs get evenly distributed across viable numbers. They source the clientele through counseling and education. Extension precedes loan sanction. Some NBFCs invest in even training the entrepreneurs. They view the requirements of the entrepreneurs comprehensively and extend all facilities under one umbrella. Their documentation procedures are simple. Appraisal and sanction take place within specified timelines without the entrepreneur having to make repeated rounds to the company.

Banks that adopt such proactive approach and lay confidence in the entrepreneur are actually more preferred destinations for the MSMEs. Banks can rationalise their interest rates and charges on the basis of portfolio risk and enterprise risk. Facilitated by the CGTMSE, the Banks can also offer low interest rates to non-collateralised loans.

Banks can also save on their capital if they enhance the MSME portfolio through the CGTMSE window while reducing the risk weights simultaneously.

Credit Needs: Policy Implications Around Enterprise Life Cycle

RBI classifies all loans to MSMEs as priority sector lending and all banks are required to extend 60 per cent of total MSME sector advances to micro enterprises. As per a recent Dun & Bradstreet report, aggregate borrowings of SMEs from both banks and NBFCs grew 17 per cent in 2017-18.

Credit risk for MSMEs is supposed to be assessed by the financing officials – whether bank or NBFC, from the points of view entrepreneur, enterprise and environment. Due diligence of the entrepreneur, technologies, products and related markets in regard to demand, and regulations and trade facilitation in regard to environment are the areas of inquest by the financing officials.

Moral hazard occurs when the borrowers of MSMEs take higher risks than lenders without support from the banks. While owners of the firms may benefit from any additional returns, in the event of firm's failure the lenders suffer disproportionately. Most MSEs suffering from inadequate working capital and untimely releases resort to external borrowings leading to such moral hazard.

MSMEs also find hard to switch lenders faced with difficulties during the growth stage of the life cycle even when benefits of switching results in lowering the costs involved. In a way, MSME lending is operating in a sellers' market.

On account of misplaced targets and staff inadequacies, routinised scrutiny of balance sheets—projected for the new enterprises and historical for the existing enterprises—and the related ratios prevailed over the qualitative areas of monitoring and supervision. This has resulted in improper assessments and untimely financial support leading to failure of enterprises and creating NPAs in banks' books. The compensations sought through collateral securities and guarantees have only provided systemic comfort. The loan books did not improve both qualitatively and quantitatively.

Loan Origination issues

Visit of entrepreneurs to the bank branches

Branches have an advances officer; he and branch manager together originate the loans. The branch manager, after a discussion with the entrepreneurs makes him fill the application form. There is no record of the rejected walk-ins at the bank branch although there are specific instructions from the RBI to that effect.

Visit of relationship managers to industry association

All public sector banks have relationship managers directly reporting to Assistant General Manager or a specific designated authority. They visit the industry associations, MSME development institutes and also clients that come through referrals. SBI, for example, has relationship managers for different districts; these generally source loan upwards to Rs 50 lakh. For smaller loans, the branch remains the only sourcing point.

Online: MSME applies for sanction of the proposals through bank website, and these account for less than 5 per cent of MSME proposals.

By and large, the MSMEs fall under the suspected category and not respected category of the clientele. Several existing entrepreneurs, who would not like to be named, mention that even their long association does not secure them higher limits of sanction even against specific work orders.

Credit Rating

The external rating is not useful as it is much lower than the banks internal rating in many cases. The rating agencies go only by certain parameters. Internal rating has the advantage of established relationship between the bank and the MSME unit and the circumstances under which a unit performed at its best or worst. Any business has risks and the profit line cannot be expected to always look northwards.

Further, banks also draw comfort from their relationship with the borrower, history of cheque bounces, collateral, etc. in pricing loans etc. These factors are usually not captured in external rating. The banks use their internal rating to price the loans. However, collateral and its nature and extent also play a role in interest rate pricing.

Diversion and siphoning of funds

Though diversion of funds has often been cited as one of the reasons for the low credit flow to the SMEs, there is a case to appreciate the constraints of the SMEs. Due to the nature of their operations and size constraints, SMEs find it difficult to efficiently manage their cash and funding liquidity risk. Lack of expertise in managing market risks often results in deploying the resources in the long-term assets. This leads to liquidity problems during episodes of cash flow problems and financial stress. The resultant disputes between the SMEs and the banks about diversion of funds lead to break-down of trust between the bank and the entrepreneur and could result in drying up of funds and ultimately sickness of the unit. The issue, therefore, requires innovative solutions.

Insistence on collateral security

As a result of asymmetric information and high-risk perception, banks primarily prefer collateral-based lending rather than cash-flow based lending while working with small-scale sector borrowers. Although banks are required to lend to MSEs without taking collateral security for loans up to Rs 10 lakh mandatorily and above Rs 10 lakh and up to Rs 200 lakh (since 2016) based on track record and financial position of the unit, the branch level officials are reluctant to assume the risk involved in non-collateralised lending. The main objective is that the lender should give importance to project viability and secure the credit facility purely on the primary security of the assets financed. The other objective is that the lender availing guarantee facility should endeavour to give composite credit to the borrowers so that the borrowers obtain both term loan and working capital facilities from a single agency.

Credit Guarantee Trust for Micro and Small Enterprises (CGTMSE)

RBI, in its Annual Report 2016, expressed concern over the over-leveraging of the corpus and the way the guarantee scheme is functioning. Information asymmetry and adverse selection on the part of member lending institutions seem to worry the regulator. Still worrisome issue is the absence of regulatory oversight on this institution. Several SME-strong economies have sound credit insurance and guarantee mechanisms and there can be no second thought on having such a robust mechanism even in our economy as MSMEs are engines of growth and cradles of innovation.

Banks' field staff, who handled just multiples of tens of accounts earlier, handle multiples of hundreds today. The government could be happy that millions of accounts are in the finance hub. But for the banks, such numbers spell danger if they are not managed well. Due diligence, monitoring and supervision have been sacrificed as a result. Moral hazard has engulfed the guarantee structure.

Guarantees in credit sector can never insure against adverse selection of the bank/FI and wilful delinquency of the borrower. They only insure genuine industry and entrepreneur failures in the normal course of business during the life cycle.

The Trust has issued cumulative guarantees to 23.23 lakh MSE loans involving an aggregate credit of Rs 1.08 trillion over the last 16 years. Its corpus grew to Rs 4,328 crore as of 31 March 2016. In all, 133 Member Lending Institutions are participating in the scheme.

The structure of the Fund is such that the government contributes four times that of SIDBI's. The Funds from this Corpus are invested in several long-term securities with accumulated returns. Any default payout is adjusted using these funds and returns from them.

Since the Corpus for the Trust is contributed by the Government of India and SIDBI, the guarantee for the leveraged loans is treated as sovereign guarantee and, therefore, under Basel II regulations, Banks are exempt from making provisions against the loans guaranteed by the CGTMSE when they become NPAs. Such exemption is available because the guarantees are also shown as contingent liabilities of the Government of India in its Budget annually.

The CGTMSE feels that it has reached a level of maturity in handling the processes enabling it to extend the cover within a week of receipt of applications as also release the claims within a fortnight, as revealed in its Annual Report 2015-16.

Although it expressed willingness to work with state governments through special schemes, Kerala—the first state that expressed willingness—had to backtrack as the CGTMSE wanted it to be a contingent liability of the state government. This condition in effect means that there is virtually no risk sharing by the CGTMSE. Further, for the state government, such provisioning would affect the FRBM. State participation whittled.

Presently, the National Credit Guarantee Trust Company under the Union Ministry of Finance has released different loan products for MUDRA, low-cost housing loans of NHC, education loans, etc. and these are on the same technology platform of CGTMSE. **CGTMSE charges a service fee of Rs 0.35 ps per cent.** In effect, the CGTMSE is managing the entire gamut of risks attached to the MSEs, retail loans under MUDRA, education and housing with no regulatory oversight. This should be naturally a cause for worry.

Other Guarantee schemes are that of the IFCI that opened exclusive cover for the entities set up for the Scheduled Castes entrepreneurs. While more than 90 per cent of MSMEs, according to the Fourth MSME Census, constitute proprietary units, and only 0.2 per cent is in the corporate domain, it is doubtful whether the scheme would ever take off.

Guarantee and Insurance mechanisms for MSME sector should have a bias to extending guarantee to the manufacturing sector. Second, the threshold levels of risk for non-collateral loans would need to increase from the existing 85 per cent to 90 per cent for the micro enterprises, i.e., for loans up to Rs 10 lakh (sanctioned limits); 80 per cent for loans up to Rs 50 lakh beyond Rs 10 lakh and 75 per cent for loans up to Rs 100 lakh beyond Rs 50 lakh. Wherever CGTMSE guarantee is obtained, the cover shall be available for both the term loans and working capital together and not either of them. Such guarantee shall be available up to 65 per cent of the sanctioned limits up to Rs 500 lakh where the Banks can cover their loans beyond Rs 100 lakh with appropriate collateral securities.

The CGTMSE has reached a level of maturity in handling the processes enabling it to extend the cover within a week of receipt of applications as also release the claims within a fortnight.

With such facilitation covering 133 Member Lending Institutions, why did the scheme not take off to the advantage of the MSEs? Although MLIs are expected to do due diligence, the pressure to cover government-sponsored schemes has led to indiscrete lending that led to a few institutions indulging in frauds. This has eroded the confidence of the CGTMSE in their MLIs to a degree. Second, in view of the large numbers in the loan ticket size of less than Rs 5 lakh, banks find the premium levied to be high eating into the cost of lending for such vulnerable groups. Second, MLIs have been lax on due diligence practices taking to armchair lending. Third, post-credit supervision and recovery management have also suffered.

MLIs preferring to take collateral either for increase/extension of the term loan/working capital would not be eligible for claim under the scheme. Further, MLI liability does not cease merely by issuing a notice under SARFAESI Act without putting the claim on primary security. The guarantee claim is also unlikely to be honoured if the annual servicing fee is in default from the MLI. The lock in period for any guaranteed account is 18 months. In case the MLI is aware that the account is likely to be NPA and chooses to apply for guarantee post facto, it will not be eligible for guarantee cover for such accounts.

A liberal approach from CGTMSE could lead to moral hazard in that banks could leverage the guarantee for firms with doubtful credentials but not verified in the beginning. Insisting on banks to file law suits against every default of MSE before claim is submitted would mean undue delay and burden on both the banks and MSEs. It has been noticed that units fit for revival and restructuring are invariably pushed to the guarantee window. This can be warded off by the CGTMSE insisting on a certificate from an independent agency like Industrial Health Clinics, wherever located, or accredited responsible consulting firms that the firms are unfit for revival for a small fee payable by the former.

Note

1. SED Report on MSMEs, 2011.

9

Clusters & Cluster Development

Cluster-based Approach

Under the cluster approach, customer focus, cost control, cross-selling and containing risk—known as 4Cs—will be taken care of. Cluster-based approach for financing the SME sector offers possibilities of reduction of transaction costs and mitigation of risk. A cluster is defined as a geographically bound concentration of similar, related or complementary businesses. A cluster-based approach to lending may be more beneficial for:

1. Dealing with well-defined and recognised groups;
2. Availability of appropriate information for risk assessment; and
3. Monitoring by the lending institution.

By way of cluster approach, SMEs can pool finance for a group of SMEs which otherwise individually may not have been able to tap the banks. This approach gives credibility to the SMEs as well as providing a cost-effective and efficient way to tap the banks for further expansion of credit in these directions.

The government has set up a number of committees to recommend measures to improve financial inclusion of MSMEs; two important reports of the Chakrabarty Committee (RBI, 2008) and Planning Commission[1] are discussed below.

The Chakrabarty Committee suggested a scheme for utilising specified NGOs for providing training-related services to tiny micro enterprises with co-funding from the Government; creation of development institutions of borrowers like cooperatives; co-funding of participation in exhibitions and marketing fairs; development of common facilities by BDS providers; and providing financial assistance for infrastructure creation; and, called for objective and quick assessment of incipient sickness and sickness in enterprises and help rehabilitation on a time-bound basis with regular monitoring schedules.

A study commissioned by the Planning Commission and carried out by the Institute of Small Enterprises and Development, has made arguments on similar lines. It has come out with a comprehensive programme of involving non-governmental actors in enterprise development programmes. More and more MFIs and NGOs need to be encouraged towards working as Business Correspondents and facilitators for banks for micro enterprises, only in identified excluded rural and semi-urban areas by necessary tax concessions etc. as suggested by the Rangarajan Committee. The banks may encourage these Business Correspondents especially in backward areas by equity participation, loans on concessional rates and other similar measures. Further, infrastructure at EDCs may be utilised for identification of the weaknesses and the areas for capacity building of the MFIs and the target clientele.

Outsourcing, as above, clubbed with credit score-based lending in small enterprises is expected to give a quantum increase in lending to micro enterprises especially in the rural and semi-urban areas where the informal channels of information are strong and the outsourcing agency being locally placed would be in a better position to assess the creditworthiness, financial strength and other factors and present the same to the bank for making a decision. The one-time cost of information as a percentage of the loan amount is expected to be less than what the banks incur today, especially in small loans.

'United we stand. Divided we fall' – the age-old adage applies in every sphere of life—in family, warfare, business, education, entertainment and collective approach. Small and medium enterprises, considering the complex situation in which they are placed, have an option in forming clusters as risk mitigation strategy.

What is a cluster?

Different countries in the world have defined clusters in their own way keeping in mind the policy framework, nature of products, technology used, and ethnic and demographical factors. However, we may understand the concept as under:

1. A cluster is a geographically bound concentration of similar related or complementary businesses with active channels for business transaction, communication and dialogue that share specialised infrastructure, labour markets and services that are faced with common opportunities and threats.
2. A cluster is a sector and geographical concentration of MSMEs faced with common opportunities and threats.
3. The product category, product range, market opportunities and identical factors like location, process, and trade practices also can be building factors for the enterprises to come together as a cluster.

Cluster approach – what it can do?

The two main challenges of an SME are: 1. to upgrade themselves from local, national to global markets; 2. meet competition through superior quality and technology upgradation. The SMEs in this approach can –

1. Access information, knowledge skills and finance
2. Have linkage with markets and suppliers
3. Correct inadequate strategies and improve organisation
4. Overcome inefficient regulations and take advantage of the existing incentives

The cluster approach can lead to:

1. Inter-firm cooperation culture
2. Cooperation + competition
3. Combines flexibility and efficiency
4. Continuous upgradation of production, markets, skills and technology
5. Increases innovation joint learning and collective efficiency.

Enhancing SME Competitiveness through Cluster Development[2]	
Deficiencies	Remedies through cluster
Nature of deficiencies in SMEs	Remedies sought through cluster initiative
Individualistic & Non-sharing	Awareness and trust building interactions among the cluster participants
Lack of collective thinking	Industry associations are associated to bring about effective idealisation and participation; networking both within and outside the cluster
High costs	Consortium approach in procurement of raw materials, contracts and financing; sharing of costs of common services
Low quality	Common testing and R & D facilities; Awareness programmes on quality management; benchmarking
Low market penetration	Product innovation; product diversification; market information and market diversification strategies & market research

Lack of or poor brand image	Brand building; brand imaging; co-branding; and brand management
Low capital, low debt and poor financial management	Improved access to debt markets; skill building in financial and accounting management; build bridges of understanding between the financing institution and entrepreneurs for better facilitation; innovation of new financial products to suit partnership the specific products and markets.
Lack of institutional supports	Institution building and building strong public-private in building product specific and general infrastructure
Lack of enthusiasm and disinterested second generation entrepreneurs	Entrepreneurship development programmes specifically designed for the cluster

Identification of Clusters

Since Cluster Development is relatively a new approach in the field of MSME Development, an inventory of clusters in the country with the information required for proper cluster selection is not available. Hence, cluster selection can be done only with secondary sources combined with expert opinion.

However, a broad guideline for selection of a potential cluster would contain elements such as location and product growth factor, whether vertical or horizontal.

The following aspects occupy a significant position in the Cluster Development frame work.

Skills Upgradation

1. Technical training of trainees
2. Training in basic drawing and designing skills of artisans

3. Training of second-level Managers in information technology
4. Training in Product diversification

Strengthening of Linkages

Participation in local/national/international trade fairs; organisation of exhibition-cum-sales; showrooms' renovation; selection criteria of directors; designers; documentation and preservation of traditional art form.

Innovative Product Development

Introduction of new technologies, innovations to indigenous technologies; adaptive and appropriate technologies could all contribute to innovative product development.

Institutional Capacity Building

Creation of specialised consortia; regular meetings of Local Associations; Specialised skills in upgrading the programmes of the rural artisans; Specialised buyer-seller meetings.

Joint participation in trade fairs with other countries

There are more than 400 SME clusters in India. These clusters are overwhelmingly dominated by small units and the share of medium enterprises in production, turnover, and employment is nominal. Some of the clusters produce 70-80 per cent of the total volume of that product manufactured in India. The Planning Commission has included this as a major initiative in SME development strategy and employment–oriented strategy. Two parallel initiatives are currently on stream – one, through the Ministry of Industry and Commerce that provides funds for infrastructure development in clusters through SPVs promoted by private or public-private partnerships and incentivises export-oriented clusters located in SEZs and AEZs and the other through the Ministry of MSME with the DCMSME as the nodal officer, which implements cluster initiatives through state governments and

Industry Associations. A number of institutions that include export houses, common service centres, non-governmental organisations/ associations have been revitalised and government officials and promoting institutions have been sensitised to the Cluster Development initiatives.

SIDBI also played a major role in the development of textile clusters initiated by the Textiles Committee in its countrywide effort. Seven state governments (Andhra Pradesh, Tamil Nadu, Karnataka, Kerala, Odisha, Madhya Pradesh and Rajasthan) have adopted cluster development within the framework of their state industrial policies with UNIDO support. Numerous nation-wide support institutions joined, most prominent among them the State Bank of India, Development Commissioners—Handicrafts and Handlooms and the Chambers of Commerce. Innovative financial practices in the Consortia (Bangalore Machine tool cluster), Entrepreneurial Development Programme in Bagru (Jaipur), introduction of ICT in Ludhiana, building bridges of understanding between the regulators and the entrepreneurs in food processing sector in Pune on quality stipulations and legal requirements are some worthy interventions so far.

Panipat produces 75 per cent of the country's total blanket output. Similarly, Ludhiana produces 95 per cent of the country's woollen knitwear, 85 per cent of the country's sewing machines and 60 per cent of the nation's bicycle and bicycle parts.

SMEs' wide range, spread over 7,500 products, offers enough scope for clusterization and agglomerate initiatives.

These clusters are estimated to contribute up to 60 per cent of India's manufactured exports. Their size in terms of number of units and quantum of output may vary, with some being so big that they produce up to 70-80 per cent of the total volume of a product (Surat and Mumbai—80 per cent in gems and jewellery; Tiruppur in Coimbatore District, Tamil Nadu—80 per cent in cotton hosiery exports). Panipat, for example, produces 75 per cent of total blankets produced in the country. Similarly, Agra with 800 registered and 6,000 unregistered small and cottage footwear production units makes 1.5 lakh pairs of shoes a day with a production value of Rs 1.3 million. Ludhiana produces 95 per cent of woollen knitwear, 85 per cent of the country's sewing machines and 60 per cent of the nation's bicycles and bicycle parts.

Lending to SME Clusters

A full-service approach to cater to the diverse needs of the SME sector may be achieved through extending banking services to recognised SME clusters by adopting a 4C approach namely, customer focus, cost control, cross-sell and contain risk. A cluster-based approach to lending may be more beneficial:

(i) In dealing with well-defined and recognised groups
(ii) Availability of appropriate information for risk assessment and
(iii) Monitoring by the lending institutions.

Clusters may be identified based on factors such as trade record, competitiveness and growth prospects and/or other cluster specific data.

In order to enable the lending institutions to take more objective decisions, an appropriate rating mechanism for designated industrial clusters may be put in place. Accordingly, a scheme may be designed jointly by CRISIL, IBA, SIDBI and SSI Associations. This would enable institutional funding to be channelised through homogenous recognised clusters. Credit rating of clusters would aid not only the lenders but also the clusters themselves by providing information on wider market opportunities for their products, strengthen negotiability and adopt improved business practices and better-quality control. Lenders, in turn, may be in a position to cross-sell their financial products through better market penetration, monitoring and information sharing.

Formulating and institutionalising rating for clusters or stand-alone SMEs (through techniques such as balanced score card or appropriate software) is a key to rapid deployment of cost-effective credit. It is important to encourage SSI Associations to take initiatives which would enable their SSI members to be rated individually or as clusters, by banks or rating agencies. SIDBI is in the process of consultation with number of banks for setting up an independent rating agency. This should be expedited and implemented.

Linking with Large Industry

There is strong evidence those SSIs which are linked as suppliers, service providers, etc. to successful large industries are usually successful ventures, in India as well as in many other countries. Such successful SSI/large industry linkages provide examples of best practices which can be aggressively extended. There are a number of corporates in India who adopt Corporate-linked SME cluster models to gain competitive advantage in local as well as global markets and derive mutual benefit. Corporate-linked SME cluster models need to be actively promoted by banks and FIs. Banks linked to large corporate houses can play a catalytic role in promoting this model. Financing SMEs linked to large corporate, covering suppliers, ancillary units, dealers, etc. would also enhance competitiveness of the corporate as well as the SME participants.

Adoption of 'Best Practices Code' for large corporates dealing with the SME sector on the lines of 'Code for Payments for large industries/ corporates', formulated by CII, would greatly help the sector regarding timely payment to SMEs. This may also enable SMEs to access better technology as well as complying with quality and environmental standards.

Cross-Selling imposes costs and reduces sanctioned limits of MSEs

Several PSBs insist on the units picking up Mutual Funds and Insurance as a precondition for either sanction of loan or enhancement of limits because of the incentives for cross-selling to the staff. There were instances where the staff offered clean loans to meet these obligations and later treated them as working capital!

Failure of marketing incentive schemes and the PSBs' cross-selling cut into the working capital upfront or loading with higher quantum of debt. Incipient sickness arising as a result is like a deformed child begging for treatment. RBI should take a serious view and introduce punitive measures on Banks that indulge in such activity to the MSME customers.

Movable Asset Registry

The then Deputy Governor of RBI, S.S. Mundra,[1] identified the four broad supply side issues: Access/Availability; Banks and Business; Collateral requirements; and Documentation. While dealing with Credit and Collateral, he has highlighted the impending initiative of setting up a Movable Asset Registry where the movable assets as opposed to fixed assets like the land and buildings that often account for most of the capital stock of MSMEs are the main securities pledged to the banks for securing their working capital. RBI in coordination with CERSAI and GoI has set up the Movable Registry. This Registry is expected to securitise the movable assets in the hands of the lender and will in effect be a risk mitigation instrument for the sector in addition to the CGTMSE cover.

Financing Receivables

For the small and medium enterprises Trade Receivable Discounting System (TReDS) has been operationalised with the RBI licensing three entities for the purpose. The objective is to create electronic Bill Factoring exchanges that would electronically accept and settle bills where the buyers and sellers should register. Unless the Government departments, PSUs (the major entities delaying payments) and corporate entities are required to transact with MSMEs mandatorily this would not be a game changer. Medium enterprises and Small enterprises with a turnover of more than Rs 100 lakh per annum would for sure benefit from this exchange. Bigger questions, however, remain: capacity building of the MSMEs on the use of this exchange and the inclination of government departments and PSUs to be members of this exchange and how soon this would happen?

Notes

1. ISED (1989): Understanding Informalism, (Cochin/New Delhi, ISED/ Planning Commission, GoI)
2. B. Yerram Raju and P.R. Mohan Nataraj (2008): Small and Medium Enterprises in India- published by the Indian Institute of Banking and Finance, Mumbai- Taxman publication (2008)

10

SMEs' Access to Capital Markets in India

It took almost a decade since the SME Exchange was formalised to see 60 floats in a month. Still the total number of listings on the SME bourses is not something that the growing Indian economy can be proud of.

In India, most SMEs operate in debt markets. The cost of raising debt for SMEs is increasingly becoming problematic both from the points of adequacy as well as timeliness and most often banks take away the umbrella in times of either too hot Sun or heavy downpour. But in a digital world simplifying businesses in the small sector also demands investments where the returns come gradually and not at the pace at which a financial institution extending credit demands. It is, therefore, necessary for the firms in the sector to look for enhancing equity.

Debt is cumbersome and equity is costly. The latter is the better choice if the SME has a modicum of discipline as creditors armed with amended SARFAESI Act 2016 and Insolvency and Bankruptcy Code are likely to be draconian. But such access demands better financial discipline, healthy balance sheets, and good governance. Scale of operation also matters for access to equity markets. Most often SMEs ask: "At what level of turnover, should I move to equity markets?" There is no answer to this question. The enterprise should have the habit of monitoring its debtors and creditors on a continuing basis and make finance a slave and not master of its operations.

"Need for Equity financing[1]

While SMEs face challenges in accessing credit, they may also lack awareness of equity as an alternate source of financing. The nascent financing requirements for a start-up are met by informal financing from friends and family. Such seed money invested in a small business is in the nature of equity but is not formally recognised as such in SMEs without a formal legal structure.

Even for start-ups that are more aware, the creation of a formalised venture often requires the aid of incubators and angel investors that provide financing and other services. Further scale-up then requires higher amount of capital, which is typically provided by venture capital funds. Apart from equity capital, the venture also needs debt for working capital.

Access to equity financing has been examined in detail in the Report of the Committee on Angel Investment and Early Stage Venture Capital (Mitra Committee), June 2012. The key issues are related to differential taxation of investments, and the need for certain enablers to expand the availability of equity capital for early stage companies.

BCB Finance Ltd (BSE) and EMERGE (NSE) are the two equity platforms. SMEs being small companies are at the beginning of their growth cycle and are also at the extreme end of the risk curve—very high levels of return are accompanied by very high levels of risk.

SMEs on the growth curve invariably look for easy access to capital. FDIs are also allowed for investing in SMEs up to 25 per cent of equity without any prior approvals. In the emerging market scenario, where mergers and acquisitions have been increasingly surfacing, firms both in India and abroad have been looking for such options for expansion. But for this to happen, SMEs should have strong equity base and the SME exchange route is a safe option to access capital markets. It is important to note that accessing FDI involves careful assessment of forex risks and sovereign risks. In the context of digitised world, be also wary of cyber risks that are increasingly looking northwards.

Facilitation for SMEs

The two distinct advantages of using dedicated SME platforms are: easy listing norms; and IPO listing norms are simple. For an investor, it becomes easier to search from segregated stocks as there will be limited number of firms. However, trading pick up has been slow. This has to improve only with the market makers using some proprietary funds only for the purpose of supporting stocks through two-way quotes on daily basis and holding a minimum specified amount of capital or stock in the SME. Confidence building in the exchange for small firms is extremely important at the moment. Minimum lot size is Rs 1 lakh. Investors need to understand SME business risks and corporate governance principles and there is need for capacity building on this count.

A minimum preparation of six months is imperative for firms to access capital through this route and hand-holding has to be done by EMERGE-like firms. BSE data till 25 November 2016 reveals that 161 firms, with a Market Cap of Rs 16,155 crore, raised Rs 1257 crore, and of them 18 (12 per cent) migrated to the Main Board. No SME has been suspended till date.

The new definition of SMEs facilitates equity financing for SMEs unable to give the guarantees traditional lenders require, by granting favourable treatment to certain investors, such as regional funds, venture capital companies and business angels without the enterprise losing its SME status.

Global experience in equity financing[2] reveals that the US, the UK, Israel, European nations, Turkey and China have worthwhile emulations for SME Equity access.

The US

Many states in the US give tax write-offs for angel investments up to US$500,000 in start-ups. The Small Business Investment Company (SBIC) under the Small Business Administration (SBA) operates as a fund of funds. It invests up to 75 per cent in a downstream venture capital (VC) funds capital, subject to a maximum of US$108 million. SBIC as on 30 September 2013 managed almost US$20 billion in private capital and SBA guaranteed leverage and commitments.

Israel

The government of Israel has directly funded incubators as well as venture funds, while also creating an environment conducive for entrepreneurship. In a decade, 1600 companies with government funding under PPP with incubators leveraged six fold from private sources, focusing on domestic capacity building for products manufactured in Israel. Under Absorption Law, government absorbs a percentage of losses that institutional investors might suffer on account of VC investments.

The government also set up a fund, YOZMA, to invest directly and also to operate as a fund of funds. Its objective was to promote technology initiatives and involvement of private venture capital in the Israeli technological sector. It can take up to 40 per cent of the total fund size and has invested more than US$200 million. It has led to 164 start-ups receiving funding, more than 50 per cent successful exits and original funds bought out or privatised within five years.

The UK

The United Kingdom has two major schemes for start-ups, Enterprise Investment Scheme (EIS) and Seed Enterprise Investment Scheme (SEIS). EIS was launched in 1994 and SEIS in April 2012. Up to 2013, as many as 20,000 firms benefited from the scheme involving GBP 9.7 billion.

Both schemes, with the same basic features, differ in quantum of tax reliefs. While EIS caters to slightly mature companies which are funded by VCs, SEIS caters to early stage companies receiving Angel Investor Funding. Income tax payers can invest in start-up companies and receive the following tax reliefs:

- Income tax relief in the tax year of investment (30 per cent relief for investments under EIS with maximum annual investment of GBP 1 million and 50 per cent relief for investments under SEIS with maximum annual investment of GBP 100,000).
- Any gains upon realisation are free of capital gains tax if shares are held for a minimum of three years. For sale before the expiry of three-year period, no capital gains tax is applicable in case

the money is re-invested in a similar EIS/SEIS eligible company. Investors can claim losses on investment up to a certain limit.[3]

Turkey

In Turkey, Business Angels are given accreditation by the Financial Markets Regulatory Department of the Treasury allowing deduction of 75 per cent of their investment from income tax.

European Union

Dependent and independent SMEs

Small and medium-sized enterprises (SMEs) are a focal point in shaping enterprise policy in the European Union (EU) and are the backbone of European economy providing majority of new jobs. The European Commission considers SMEs and entrepreneurship as key to ensuring economic growth, innovation, job creation, and social integration in the EU. However, in official statistics, SMEs can currently only be identified by employment size as enterprises with fewer than 250 persons employed. This is a big category and encompasses enterprises with different ownership structures and varying numbers of employees and levels of economic activity.

- Independent Enterprise: an enterprise which, according to the business register (BR), is not controlled by another enterprise (neither domestic nor foreign), and at the same time, it does not itself control another enterprise (neither in the country of residence nor abroad);
- Dependent Enterprise: an enterprise which, according to the BR, is controlled by another enterprise (either domestic or foreign), and/or, it controls itself another enterprise (either in the country of residence or abroad). Dependent enterprises belong to an enterprise group.

The Programme for the Competitiveness of Small and Medium-sized Enterprises (COSME) runs from 2014 to 2020, with a planned budget of EUR 2.5 billion.[4]

China

SMEs in China are defined in a complex way reckoning employment, turnover and assets with multiple classification—manufacturing, construction, wholesale and retail trade, transport, post and hotels and restaurants. Thresholds vary according to classification as per SME Promotion Law of 2003. According to China Statement Year Book, 2015, 97.9 per cent of all enterprises are SMEs and the rest are State-owned Enterprises (SOEs). Assets of SMEs constitute 53.4 per cent of the total assets contributing to 53 per cent of total revenue, 58 per cent of GDP and 68 per cent of exports.

However, 66 per cent of the SMEs find it difficult to access institutional finance. The access to short term capital is even worse at only 4.7 per cent of the total requirement. In China informal finance is not illegal. They are also not regulated by the Central Banking Regulatory Authority.[5]

Equity finance funding in India

While Government of India placed with SIDBI Rs 10,000 crore benefits to the early stage entrepreneurial ecosystem covering incubators, angel investor groups and venture capital investors particularly for the manufacturing SMEs are found wanting. This explains the reason for tardy manufacturing sector growth and limping Make in India efforts. The asset intensive manufacturing firms are generally not serviced by angels and VCs.

Promote equity investment by angel investors/ venture funds

There is a need to recognise and incentivise early stage investor classes by a system for recognition/accreditation of angel investors. Qualified investors, as may be determined by regulatory authorities, including high net-worth individuals (HNIs), corporates and other investors in such early stage funds could be given incentives. The incentives could include tax credits, tax pass through limited liability partnerships structures, etc. for angel investors. They can also be provided tax incentives similar to the ones given in the UK, including 50 per cent tax rebate for investments up to Rs 1 crore, no capital gains tax where investment is for a minimum period of three years and provision to claim loss on investment up to a certain limit.

To promote domestic investment, the government may permit and encourage pension funds, insurance companies and banks to invest a small part of their corpus in early stage VC funds to encourage domestic funding and introduce a level playing field for domestic equity financing as compared to foreign investors at the stage of investment, and as compared to mutual funds and listed equity on the treatment of capital gains by rationalising the tax structure.

There are anomalies in Section 56(2) (vii-b) of the Income Tax Act regarding fixation of fair market value of the shares in the case of equity investment company, say, NBFC that is operating with a widely held corpus fund with promotional contribution of 10–30 per cent from the state/Union government. Usually such early stage companies do not get revenues or profits during the sourcing year. A large proportion of the capital invested in such start up stage companies is liable to be taxed under the head 'income from other sources'. Application of this provision to only domestic and not foreign companies is another anomaly. These need corrections if the government is serious about encouraging SME Equity Markets.

It is, therefore, recommended that the current exemption under Section 56(2) (vii-b) of the Act which is applicable in respect of investments received by a venture capital undertaking from a venture capital company or a venture capital fund be extended to:

- Resident financial/angel/VC investors with appropriate carve outs, by way of checks and balances, in respect of promoters and their relatives so as to prevent any 'tax avoidance' scenario. It is also desirable to allow tax pass-through benefit under Section 10(23FB) of the Income Tax Act to all categories of investment funds registered with SEBI and with the RBI as NBFCs.
- The Mitra Committee recommends that the government should meet a part of expenditure of SMEs incurred by them in the

initial listing of their equity on the SME exchanges. This part reimbursement of listing expenditure could either be limited up to 50 per cent of the total listing expenditure or Rs 10 lakh, whichever is lower.

- The Committee recommends that the Government should provide tax exemption for the investments in IPOs of SME companies under Section 80C of the Income Tax Act, 1961 within the overall prevailing ceiling limit of Rs 1,50,000.

The Mitra Committee recommends establishing a separate 'SME Equity Investment Fund' by the Ministry of MSME to be managed by a professionally run entity of fund managers. The government may also introduce a provision for Special Purpose Vehicle (SPV) to allow a group of angel investors to come together as an SPV and then invest in manufacturing start-ups. Even though angel investments are generally in a group, there is no provision to create an SPV for the same, so all individuals have to invest separately, leading to a large number of shareholders, which becomes an impediment for raising further funding from institutional investors.

Further, at the time of exit the same capital gains tax regime may be provided for investments by angel groups and VC funds as is provided to mutual funds which invest in companies listed on stock exchanges.

Many of the start-ups fail and need to fold up efficiently and quickly to arrest losses and limit liabilities. To ensure that this is not a discouraging factor for starting and investing in risky but innovative enterprises, the process of closing a business needs to be made more logical and smoother for businesses. The MSME Ministry needs to take into consideration the emerging investment environment as a visionary and convince the FM the need for more incentives for manufacturing start-ups among the SMEs. In fact, it would make lot of sense for the Ministry to recognise those small enterprises moving to bourses as equivalent to start-ups as they suffered for long years in a stifling regulatory and financial environment.

Notes

1. "Report of the Committee to examine the Financial Architecture of MSMEs," February 2015, Ministry of Finance, Government of India, New Delhi (p.45-50)
2. "Report of the Committee on Angel Investment & Early Stage Venture Capital, 2012", Government of India, Planning Commission

   http://planningcommission.nic.in/reports/genrep/rep_eco2708.pdf
3. ibid
4. "Eurostat Statistics Explained: Entrepreneurship - statistical indicators," November 2018, https://ec.europa.eu/eurostat/statistics-explained/index. php?title=Entrepreneurship_-_statistical_indicators#Small.2C_medium-sized_and_large_enterprises
5. Richard Hoffmann, "Small And Medium Enterprises (SMEs) In China," *Ecovis Beijing*, 4 July 2017, https://ecovis-beijing.com/smes-china/

11

Managing Non-Performing Assets

Non-performing assets are those that stop yielding return on the assets for the lending institution at the defined thresholds by the RBI. Classifying the asset as NPA has the consequence of the bank having to provide for losses in its profit and loss statement, which in turn leads to erosion in the capital to the extent of provision. The owners of the bank have to make good such capital in conformity with RBI regulations founded on Basel Accord. In so far as enterprise is concerned, such declaration would close the lending window of the bank. Such action would also lead to the enterprise losing its hold on the debtors. Thus the enterprise is double hit. Most banks have been ordained by the RBI to classify the assets as Special Mention Accounts the moment the enterprise is stressed. The remedies suggested by the RBI are: corrective action; handholding; restructure; revive; and recover. Delayed sanctions, delayed release of sanctioned limits even for running units, and lack of time for counselling and mentoring MSMEs in particular, efforts to cushion them through collateral securities have all been the sources of NPAs in this sector.[1]

Distressed assets

Distressed assets in the manufacturing sector have become a cause of concern. The MSME Ministry vide its circular dated 2 June 2015 issued guidelines on revival and restructuring of sick but viable enterprises and incipient sick enterprises to all the banks and state governments for compliance. Recognising the need for improving the environment for the revival of the assets or sale of such assets to Asset Reconstruction Companies (ARCs), foreign investments have been allowed. The 'going concern' concept is yet to sink in the minds of the financial institutions in order that the prevailing sickness in manufacturing sector does not stand in the way of welcoming new units of size and scalability.

RBI statistics show that stressed assets in Indian banking have reached the alarming level of 16 per cent of the total assets. However, MSMEs, suffering a cascading effect of their elder brothers incorporates as vendors, are at the fringe with around 8 per cent. The extent of 'wilful default' as defined by the RBI and the contribution of 'financial illiteracy' of MSMEs cannot be established by data. Hidden or undisclosed reasons for NPAs in banks' books have been narrated in a few research studies that include CII, FICCI, ASSOCHAM, CAB, etc., but they had no institutional solutions.

Year	(In Million)	(In Billion)	**Credit O/S Growth Rate(%)**	(In Billion)	**Growth in NPAs(%)**
	No. of Accounts	**Amount of Outstanding**		**NPAs**	
1991	4.68	164	NA	NA	NA
2010	8.73	3,640	95	127	NA
2011	9.3	4,845	25	153	20
2012	9.86	5,277	8	195	27
2013	11.23	6,848	23	304	56
2014	12.4	8,461	19	NA	NA
2015	13.8	9,612	12	NA	NA
2016	20.5	9,957	3	708	NA
2017	23.2	10,701	7	828	17
2018	25.9	11,494	7	910	10

Source: Country Specific MSME Report, KPMG-CII Report 2015

The above table reveals that MSME credit moved by 95 per cent in the first decade of liberalisation. Post 2014, when 'Make in India', 'Start-Up India' and liberalised investment policies were given a big push, enigmatically, the growth in MSME sector has been on the steady decline settling at 7 per cent during 2017 and 2018. Growth in NPAs during the last two years has been high due to the cascading effect of the corporate sector NPAs as most MSMEs are vendors to those corporate sector entities.

Banks' efforts in reducing non-performing assets by various channels such as Lok Adalats, Debt Recovery Tribunals (DRTs) and invoking SARFAESI Act provisions reveal:

1. By 31 March 2016, number of cases referred to various courts, DRT, SARFAESI and Lok Adalat have increased nearly 2 times from 2014-15 in both SCB and PSB.
2. SCB cases increased to 46,54,753 from 31,55,672 (2014-15) while the PSB cases referred increased to 44,23,080 from 27,81,552 (2014-15) indicating that the private sector banks recourse to the above legal mechanisms reduced by 1,42,447 firms.

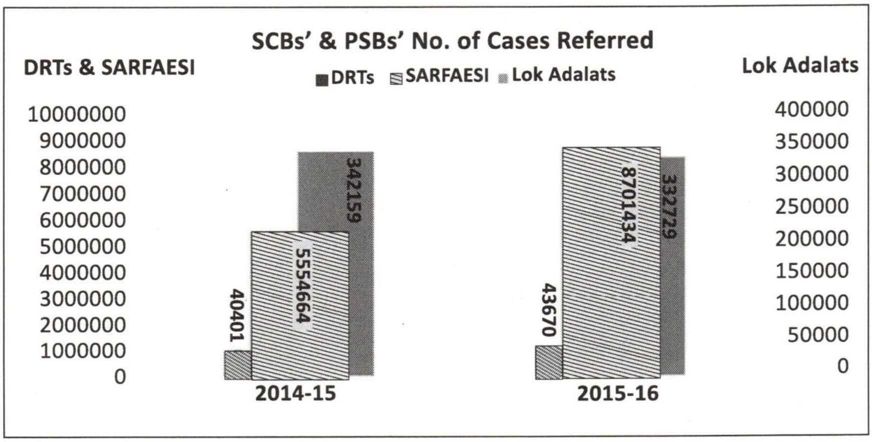

3. Recovery of NPA has decreased in both SCB and PSB in 2015-16, Gap between amount involved and amount recovered is large as given below:

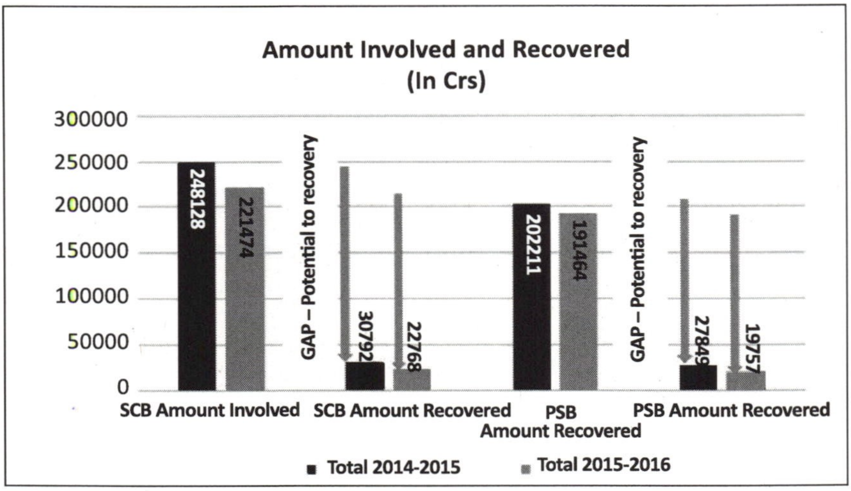

4. NPA recovery has gone down in 2015-16 from 2014-15 as shown above.
5. Banks took recourse to all the available channels for recovering NPAs.

Chart below indicates that recovery through DRT and Lok Adalat has improved from previous year whereas recourse to SARFAESI declined by 52 per cent from Rs 25,600 crore in 2014-15 to Rs 13,179 crore in 2015-16.

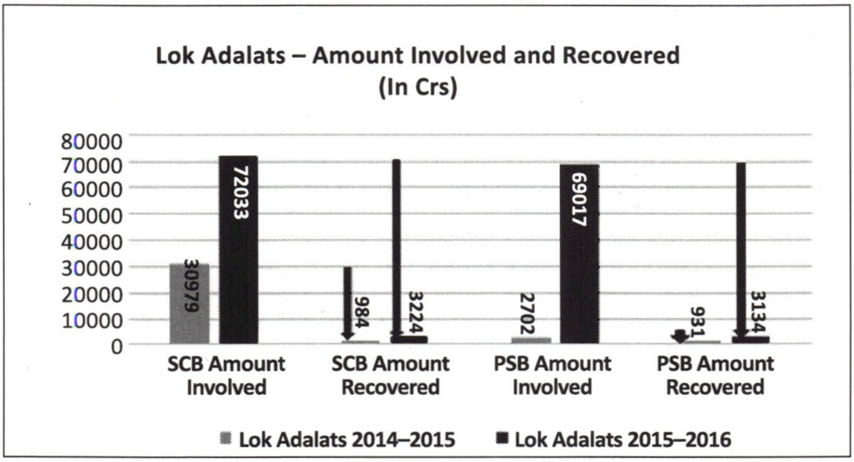

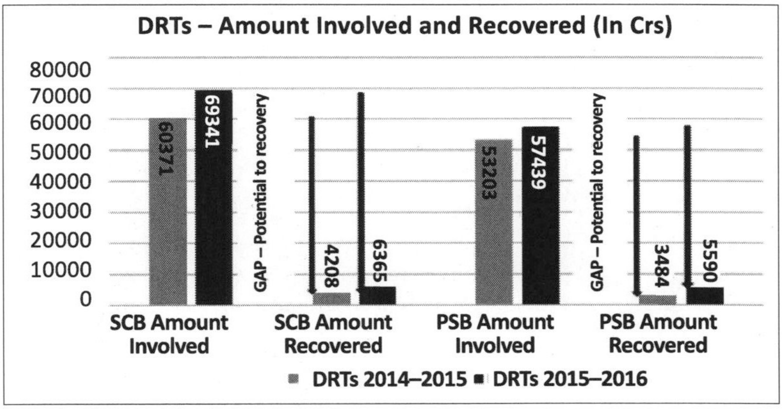

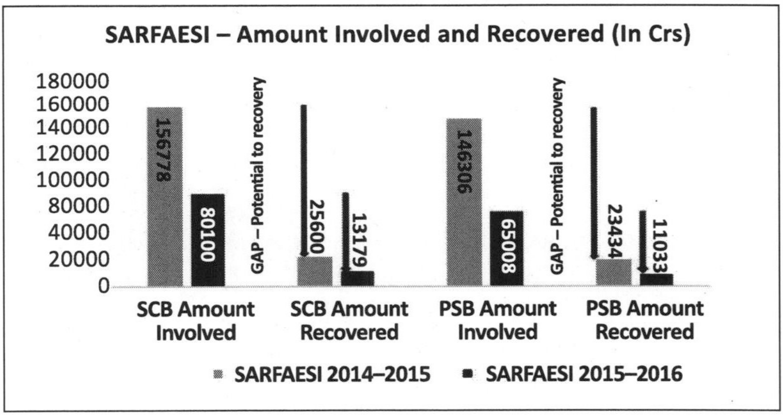

There is large gap between the amount involved and amount recovered in the SARFAESI channel. Percentage of recovery across SCBs and PSBs showed a decline from 12.14 and 13.77 in 2014-15 to 10.28 and 10.32, respectively, in 2015-16.

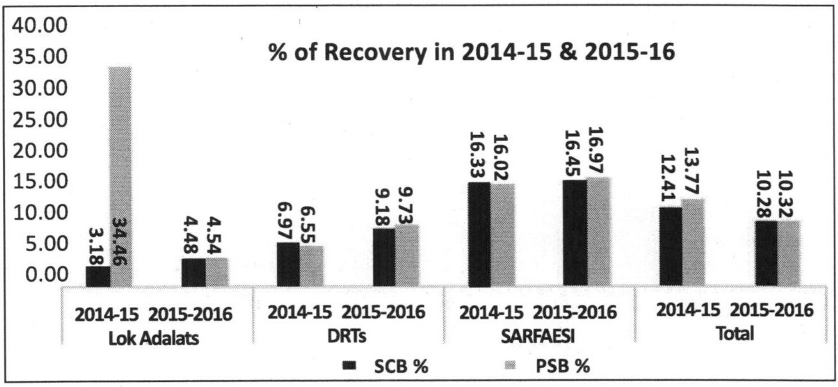

Banks can proactively solve the NPAs in MSE sector if they keep their eyes and ears open. Impact of sectoral failures caused by economic downturn both within and outside the country is available in the periodic assessments of various organisations indicated above. Similarly, they are also aware of which of the large and medium enterprises are postponing payments to their vendors, viz., MSEs. In both the instances banks can proactively provide succour to the weaklings in the industry through the periodic rescheduling of repayments when they will continue to be treated as standard assets if they are able to pay up the interest obligation. This is not to be treated as revival effort but a survival effort.

In all other cases, revival as per the RBI directives can be done in good time. It is imprudent for a bank to wait for the account to become NPA to attempt revival process as is sometimes; some banks are choosing to do. Alert banks can significantly reduce the NPAs of MSEs.

Sick Units

A unit or enterprise is considered sick when any of its borrowed accounts has become a doubtful advance as defined by RBI i.e. principal or interest in respect of any of its borrowed accounts has remained overdue for a period exceeding 90 days and there is an erosion in the net worth due to accumulated cash losses to the extent of 50 per cent or more of its peak net worth in the preceding accounting years subject to the provision that the unit has completed one full year of commercial production or 30 per cent or more of its peak net worth in the preceding accounting years in case of reference made by its financing bank or financial institution and subject to the provision that the unit has completed one year of commercial production.

CAUSES OF SICKNESS

The causes of sickness can be broadly divided into two categories, namely, internal causes and external causes.

Internal Causes

i) Management: Dishonesty and lack of integrity; lack of managerial skills; death, removal or non-availability of key personnel, dissension among partners/Directors, absentee Management; delay in project implementation improper and/ unplanned expansion of the projects.

ii) Finance: Diversion of working capital to create fixed assets; Acquisition of disproportionately high current assets; resorting to costly outside borrowing faculty costing and pricing; bad receivables and management; development expenditure for new products disproportionate to expected cash accruals; interlocking of funds in sister concerns; cost-overruns; booking large orders involving long delivery schedules at fixed price.

iii) Production: Poor labour productivity, outdated technology, frequent machine failures, lack of withdrawal of know-how, poor quality control, technology too sophisticated to be managed under-utilisation of capacity; no quality control of inputs like raw material etc.

iv) Personnel: Lack of skilled labour, high cost of labour, labour unrest.

v) Marketing: Dependence on one or very few customers, no product range, lack of understanding of customer needs; smaller area of operation, poor quality of the production, poor distribution, promotion and advertisements, market far away involving high cost of transportation.

vi) Entrepreneurship qualities: Lack of entrepreneurial qualities or risk-taking abilities in the promoters.

External Causes

a) Finance: Inadequate or delayed bank finance, repayment of term loans, inadequate start-up period for repayment of loans.

b) Production: Raw material shortage, lack of adequate supply of utilities like power, water etc., and problems with ancillaries

c) Marketing: Competition from big concerns; unscrupulous purchases and sales by others, recession in the market, market highly brand-loyal, and introduction of substitutes by competition in the market, changing styles or tastes of customers.

d) Miscellaneous: Government decisions like export /import policy excise duty, ban on product concession/subsidies allotment of raw material etc.

Additional Measures for MSME Development

In addition to the schemes operated for SME promotion development, there are a few additional measures which have been undertaken in the recent past or are presently under different stages of implementation, which are expected to have a long-term positive impact on the promotion and development of SMEs. Some of them are: enacting a law to set up Limited Liability Partnership firms; proposals to enact a Goods and Services Tax Act to remove the anomalies in the VAT and to facilitate easier movement of manufactured goods across the country. The other measures that deserve attention of the Government sooner than later are:

1. Information Asymmetry can be minimised if the DICs are strengthened by provision of modern IT-enabled communication facilities and re-training of human resources available with these institutions.
2. States should be supported by the Central government to set up Industrial Health Clinics and make operational appropriate schemes for the rehabilitation of units temporarily rendered sick due to circumstances beyond their control. The RBI/Finance Ministry should issue necessary orders in this regard so that discretion at the field level, whether by the field formations or by banks is ruled out.
3. The Government should infuse funds in industrial estates which are currently in a state of decay and neglect and upgrade them to 'Industrial Townships'.
4. Government should strengthen the equity base of NSIC to give a demand side impetus to MSME enterprises in addition to preferential procurement and volume stipulations enunciated earlier. Government should also consider earmarking funds

to the tune of Rs 15 billion, within the enhanced investment package proposed above, to support clean technology initiatives of different ministries involved with MSME growth.

5. The concept of business incubators in educational institutions of repute should be encouraged by setting aside Rs 10 billion within the overall package set out.
6. Legal and regulatory structures: The legal and regulatory structures and provisions affecting the MSME sector that could be taken up in the medium term (1-3 years) are: legal options should be developed for the securitisation of *trade credit receivables* and for the promotion of *factoring services*. One hopes that the steps taken by RBI in this regard recently would address the main financial risk of the MSMEs, i.e., cash flow mismatches.
7. Wide publicity to be given to new formats like Limited Liability Partnerships and Single Person Companies, which provide MSMEs with an interim solution in their move from the 'informal' to the 'formal' economy.
8. Insolvency legislation should be comprehensively reviewed in recognition of the reality of the global market where enterprises continuously get created and destroyed.

Labour laws need simplification especially those applicable to enterprises in the MSME sector, since the transaction costs for complying with these laws is disproportionately high for these units. While some steps have been taken by the Labour Ministry in this regard, the Task Force has recommended a single and comprehensive legislation for MSMEs with up to 40 workers. At the same time, keeping in view the large size of the unorganised sector within MSMEs, the task force recommended that labour welfare related matters should be focused on more rather than legislation by, inter alia, use of the recently promulgated Unorganised Workers Social Security Act, 2008.

Viability Norms: Rehabilitation Package

A unit can be regarded as potentially viable if it were in a position after implementing a relief package spread over a period not exceeding five years from the commencement of the package from banks, financial institutions, government (Centre/state) and other agencies concerned as may be necessary to continue to service its repayment obligations as agreed upon including those becoming part of the package without the need for such concessions after the aforesaid period. The repayment for the restructured debt (past) should not exceed seven years from the date of the implementation of the package. In the case of tiny/ decentralised sector units, the period of reliefs/concessions repayments of debts which were hitherto two years/three years respectively have been revised so as not to exceed five and seven years respectively. As in the case of other SSI units based on the norms specified above, it will be for the banks, and financial institutions to decide whether a sick unit is potentially viable or not. Viability of a unit identified as sick should be decided quickly and made known to the units and others concerned at the earliest. The rehabilitation package should be fully implemented within six months from the date the unit is declared as potentially viable/viable. While identifying and implementing the rehabilitation package, Banks/Financial institutions should do holding operation for a period of six months. This will allow the units to draw funds from the accounts at least to the extent of their deposit of sale proceeds during the period of such holding operations.

Some of the state governments like Gujarat, Uttar Pradesh, Andhra Pradesh and Maharashtra have constituted special committees with the Commissioner of Industries as the Convenor to review at shorter intervals the grant of concessions and other measures for rehabilitation. These committees examine the viability issues collectively in the presence of entrepreneurs affected by sickness and the Industry Associations. Collective wisdom, however, did not many a time deliver timely solutions.

Viability norms in general

1) The financing Bank/Institution must participate in the revival programme, offer matching sacrifice and continue to provide required working capital to the sick units.
2) Viability of the units is established in consultation with the Bank/Appraisal agency.

3) In case of a limited company net worth means the sum total of paid-up capital and free reserves. In case of a partnership/proprietary concern net worth means the sum total of partners/proprietor's capital and free reserves.

Free Reserves: Created out of profits and share premium account but does not include reserves created out of revaluation of assets, written-back depreciation and under amalgamation provisions. Bank means any public sector bank, district cooperative bank, urban cooperative bank and any other bank, which is a scheduled bank in terms of the second schedule to the Reserve Bank of India Act.

Financial Institutions: Means those that deal with SSI: SIDBI, State Finance Corporation or any other Institution which is authorised under any law to advance terms loans to industrial units.

Some identified areas of intervention

Expert groups and committees who have studied the various aspects of rehabilitation have identified same areas of policy interventions both at state and Central levels for implementation.

1. Renovation of infrastructure
2. Clusterization
3. Marketing services
4. Quality testing services and Human Resource
5. Exemption in stamp-duty and reduction of registration charges

Natural calamities: Units could have been affected by cyclones, floods, tsunami or holocaust or such other natural calamities. While general insurance could come to rescue to some degree, it is not always possible for the units to recover to normal production under such circumstances. There could be corrosion problems affecting the quality of production in the post-calamity situation. There could be some social responsibilities to be taken care; there could be serious damage to the work-in-process. Such situations demand out-of-the-box solutions. New machinery may be needed; raw material in the stores and spares could also need replacement. The Banks should quickly come to the rescue of the unit to perform all these tasks so that the unit commences quickly without losing the market.

The other area of sickness is the failure of parent units (in case of ancillaries), disturbance in environment setting up of too many similar units creating excess capacity affecting viability of existing units.

Preventive Measures

A primary preventive measure is to preserve health by removing the precipitating causes and determinants of departures from good health. To put it in epidemiological terms the aim of primary prevention is to reduce the incidence of disease and injury. Eliminating the causative agents can do this: for example, small pox virus by pasturing raw milk to kill the pathogenic organism found in it.

Secondary prevention is to detect and correct departures from good health as early as possible. In other words, to reduce the prevalence of disease and disability we can often accomplish this with screening products that detect disease before it is manifested by symptoms or signs. Screening needs to be combined with counselling about reduction of risks to health if it is to be fully effective. Health promotion is defined as the process of enabling people to increase control over and improve their health. An individual or group must be able to identify and realise the aspiration to satisfy needs and to change or cope with environment. Health is a resource for everyday life, a positive concept emphasising social and personal resources involving physical capabilities.

It is difficult for anybody to counter the statement: 'Prevention is better than cure'. But when sickness fully overtakes a person, one has to reach to both medical and surgical treatment for purposes of cure. It is also common knowledge that such treatment should be timely and at the hands of a competent doctor. Proper diagnosis should precede such treatment. The analogy seems perfect when we apply it to industry. Cases are not wanting where the doctor administered a wrong medicine. Diagnostic studies have revealed interesting dimensions to the problem of sickness in the units:

1. Some MSME entrepreneurs took advantage of all the facilities offered by every agency, governments, financial institutions and markets and misused the assistance.
2. The mushroom growth of bogus entrepreneurs can be avoided by alertness of sponsoring agencies and financial institutions by two-level screening.
3. There are instances of entrepreneurs who have set up units on their assured capability to access markets in the government sector through political connections and the moment the political friends were out of power the assumptions failed and the units collapsed.

Reliefs and Concessions

Some fiscal and non-fiscal measures under consideration of a few state governments:

1. Most of the surplus land be allowed to be sold/mortgaged;
2. Labour department should undertake to settle labour disputes, if any, to ensure success of rehabilitation package;
3. Interest subsidy up to 5 per cent to be given to each unit on working capital; and
4. Various departments and agencies should extend the following reliefs and concessions

RBI guidelines of 17 March 2016 suggested forming Zonal Committees by banks and ever since, both formation of committees and their functioning did not yield the expected results in revival of MSEs. On 1 January 2019, RBI directed the Banks to restructure all the standard assets in SMA 0-2 categories before March 2020 as a preventive measure for bulging NPAs. However, following aspects need reconsideration by the RBI.

1. The frame work is applicable only to SMA accounts and not for accounts which turned NPA.

2. SMA 2 accounts should be referred to the committee by the branch manager.

   Guidelines fail to mention when this reference should be made.

   The Committee has to take up the case within five working days.

   This is not happening. The committee meetings happen generally once a month

   It is also not certain that branch managers are referring all the SMA 2 CASES to the Committee. The Number of SMA accounts are very large as per the data of SLBC.

3. Constitution of the Committee:
   a. The Regional and Zonal heads may have to chair several meetings in a month, where the bank branches are spread over more than one district.
   b. Representative of the state government is not invariably attending the meeting.
   c. The banks may include the specialist institutions like the Industrial Health Clinics in the Committee.

4. The time frame prescribed is as follows:
   a. Committee to meet after receiving the application – 5 days
   b. Committee to notify the concerned enterprise – 5 days
   c. Enterprise to respond with information – 15 days
   d. Committee to send the notice to statutory creditors – regarding their claims
   e. And time given to them for responding – 15 days
   f. Total time taken so far – more than 40 days (without counting time taken for sending the notice in 'd' above)
   g. Committee to take a decision within 30 days of convening its first meeting. How is it possible?
   h. The SMA 2 account becomes NPA in 30 days' time. So, an SMA 2 account referred to Committee turns NPA at least 5 days before Committee decides.

   i. If a TEV study taken up it further delays the process, by which time the account becomes NPA long before. What will be the classification of the account on rectification or restructuring?

5. The Corrective Action Plan (CAP) mentions only Rectification or Restructuring. The latter requires a TEV study.

   There should be scope for a revival, without going into the process of TEV study in all simple cases and small accounts (micro units). The units which are already under stress will have to bear the additional costs of TEV study and if fresh finance is prescribed, then have to bring in almost all cases 25 per cent as margin.

   It is good that provision is made for the unit to borrow, secured or unsecured loans. Provision should be made that the bank should share the charge on the additional asset being created on *pari-passu* basis, with the lending entity.

6. In case of small accounts, up to Rs 10 crore, the responsibility is given to the branch head, without any simple and clear instructions. In their absence, branch heads either do not take up the exercise or simply apply the same principles as prescribed for bigger accounts.

One-time settlement as part of restructuring package

CDR mechanism allows one-time settlement option as a part of the restructuring package in order to bring more flexibility in the exit option to the lenders who are no more interested in continuing their exposure in the corporate entity. Facility of OTS as part of restructuring on the pattern of CDR mechanism would also be extended to SMEs borrower having facilities from multiple banks. The question of OTS option as part of restructuring doesn't arise in the case of borrowers having facilities from a single bank.

PUMPS SINK

Suman Engineering (Pvt) Ltd.

This is a diesel pump manufacturing unit located in Nellore district. It is a closely held company among the family members. The Managing Director, Prashant Kumar Reddy, is a self-motivated entrepreneur and has refined his production capabilities through his frequent visits to Coimbatore—the hub of machinery manufacturing activity. His market was mostly restricted to Nellore and Prakasam districts. As was wont with the nature of such business activity, the unit went on giving credit facilities to the dealers. The pumps manufactured by the unit had ISI certification and accreditation from the Government of Andhra Pradesh for supply to farmers under various government-sponsored projects. They have contracted term loan from SFC and working capital from SBI. Their account got blocked in the post-1999 cyclone and the SBI has settled the dues in 2002-03 under OTS of RBI. It has approached the APSSIRS for settlement of dues with the APSFC. The APSFC refused for such a settlement. But later, when the industry approached the SFC authorities, they have agreed for a settlement but failed to communicate to the District Office. The District Office of the SFC announced in the Press, that along with some other units, this unit also was due for auction. This announcement has not damaged the negotiated settlement process but has also depressed the sale price of the asset Reddy wanted to sell for honouring his commitment to SFC. The entrepreneur frowned on the unwarranted act of indiscretion. He has groomed his two sons into Engineering and Accounts careers for becoming the second-generation entrepreneurs. His ambitious future plan for succession is set at naught by the APSFC. Reddy is now the President of Federation of SMEs India, Hyderabad fighting the cause of sick enterprises.

Entrepreneurial responsibility

Entrepreneurial responsibility is of great significance in any rehabilitation effort. The entrepreneur should do the soul searching as to where he has faltered in the management and put in efforts to set right. It is important that this effort is visible to the financing agency. The confidence that the financing agency gets regarding the abilities of the unit to implement the rehabilitation package is of great importance. Some of the steps that the unit should take in this regard:

1. Maintain transparency in all the transactions;
2. Keep the bank informed of all the steps being taken;
3. Mobilise as much low-cost resources as possible from friends and relatives who could be having confidence in your abilities to run the enterprise successfully;
4. Look at the market; how it is moving; is it price sensitive; or brand sensitive; is it spatial in character; then measure up the requirements for rehabilitation and present before the financing institution;
5. Revalue your securities;
6. Invest on recovery of dues from all sundry debtors to nearly 100 per cent;
7. Go to the financing institution with a package of your own contribution in rehabilitation;
8. Seek professional guidance or guidance from the banker himself on designing a rational cash flow projection for the next five years;
9. If required, as in most cases, induct new management; induct new partners; or even go for reorganisation of the business structure so that investor confidence would increase and finally;
10. Do not commit on what is not probable and lose credibility further. Own your faults and show keenness for immediate corrections.

SARFAESI Act

The Securitisation and Reconstruction of Financial Assets and Enforcement of Security Interest (SARFAESI) Act, 2002 is a powerful instrument in the hands of the banks and financial institutions (FIs) as secured creditors. This Act helps them enforce securities held as collateral to loans disbursed by them should such loans turn out as non-performing assets (NPAs) during the currency of the loan without interference from the Courts. Section 13 of the Act gives power to the secured creditor even to evict the tenant. It is our observation that the banks have been overenthusiastic in taking recourse to SARFAESI Act provisions as a first resort of recovering the micro, small and medium enterprises (MSME) loans, mostly violating guidelines of Reserve Bank of India (RBI).

The entire process under the Act involves several factors of fairness and technicalities. During our interactions with the borrowers and banks in the State Level Inter-Institutional Sub-committee (SLIIC), we have noticed the banks jumping into coercive actions throwing overboard the due processes. It is surprising that tech-savvy systems of banks have not put in the measured timelines before pressing the red button to put the credit traffic of the MSMEs on halt.

RBI's timelines are as follows:

- ❖ If the account does not reflect credits into the account, 90 days preceding the date of balance sheet of the firm, it is treated as NPA. Temporary deficiencies like late/ non-submission of stock statements or balance outstanding exceeding the drawing power, non-renewal of limits should not get categorised as NPA.
- ❖ If the borrower does not pay three instalments continuously after 90 days but up to 12 months, the account becomes sub-standard and NPA. Section 13 (2) empowers the Bank/FI to serve notice to the borrower for taking possession of the assets held as security for the money lent by it. But there is precursor to this action: The Bank/FI shall serve notice to the borrower to discharge his full liabilities within 60 days from the date of notice that should also detail out the legal consequences and penal provisions.

Going by these two directions under the Act, the borrower should be getting at least 12 months' time before the bank could proceed against the defaulting MSMEs.

If the borrower becomes a 'wilful defaulter' as defined by the RBI Master Circular on wilful defaulters vide RBI circular (RBI/2014-15/73 DBR.No.CID.BC.57/20. 16.003/2014-15 dated 1 July 2015) SARFAESI Act proceedings can be issued even without notice to the borrower.

Who is a wilful defaulter?

- ❖ Deliberate non-payment of the dues despite adequate cash flow and good net worth;
- ❖ Siphoning off funds to the detriment of the defaulting unit;
- ❖ Assets financed either not been purchased or been sold and proceeds have been misutilised;
- ❖ Misrepresentation / falsification of records;
- ❖ Disposal / removal of securities without bank's knowledge;
- ❖ Fraudulent transactions by the borrower.

Banks/ FIs throwing overboard these norms, classify all the MSME NPAs as wilful defaulters to apply the SARFAESI lever. As per the Act, valuation of the asset has to be done and notify that valuation to the borrower before issuing public notice for auction of property. Bank must give 30 days' notice to the borrower regarding its right to proceed against the mortgaged property if he does not pay up the entire principal and interest.

However, we have noticed that in most cases all the above timelines are followed more in breach with impunity by the banks. For example, a public sector bank (PSB) branch proceeded with sale of property within 15 days of declaring the asset as NPA. They have also fixed a reserve price without consulting the impugned borrower or without taking into consideration any objections raised by the borrowers as required under Section 13(3)(A) and proceed for auction of the properties. This is the case with most collateralised MSME NPAs. On top of this, in Jammikunta town, Telangana, the bank has also engaged agents for enforcing coercive recovery measures.

In quite a few other cases, the banks sold off assets to asset restructuring companies (ARCs). Here the process is that the bank bundles a few NPAs and sells them off at a discount, which is not disclosed either to the borrower or to the SLIIC sub-committee. Although it may be in order for the bank to entertain request of the enterprise under one-time settlement (OTS) within the rules of the RBI, its preference is to transfer to ARC at a far lesser price than OTS would have gone to the bank.

Electric Transformers Fused

Messrs Jagadamba Transformers, a partnership firm, was slapped notice under SARFAESI Act after the bank declared as NPA even as it has offered adequate collateral security to back the outstanding amount of loan. When our accredited consultant went into details the following details surfaced: The partners were not financially literate. At the suggestion of the PSB Relationship Manager at the financing branch, a new partner was inducted with full powers to operate on the accounts of the firm. A scrutiny of accounts revealed without reference to the work orders excess withdrawals were allowed on four occasions, each time of the order of Rs 40-50 lakh and this amount was siphoned off into either other branch accounts or with other bank. The irregularity was later approved through submission of a fudged balance sheet created by the third partner. On two occasions, the irregularity was remitted back into the account by way of transfer of funds from another account of a different branch that was also being operated by this third partner. To the ill-luck of the firm, 2011-13 was a bad patch with agitations and power cuts. This account in the process became NPA. The bank lost no time to declare the account as wilful defaulter and served notice under SARFAESI Act.

In 2015 when the unit approached the branch with work orders from the Telangana TRANSCO requesting for providing the needed EMIs, the bank refused and said that the accounts cannot be operated and the matter is now with AGM, Stressed Accounts Recovery Branch. Repeated rounds of discussions by the unit were of no avail. The unit had under those circumstances approached the Commissioner of Industries for placing before the SLIIC.

At the SLIIC the bank officials did not disclose the real reasons for proceeding against the unit except mentioning that the unit has committed a fraud on the account hiding most of the information that we could get on detailed investigation. The bank has also chosen to hide the fact that they have filed a CBI inquiry against the Relationship Manager for his collusion with the drawing partner of the account. They also did not mention the fact that the unit's deposits maturing at different points of time to the tune of Rs 51 lakh are held by them. They also did not mention in the SlIIC that the unit has dismissed the partner and reconstituted partnership. The bank has chosen to arbitrarily close the accounts and also proceeded to wind up a well-functioning unit.

The unit since its inception had an excellent record of producing transformers of approved quality standards and not a single guarantee devolved on the bank. Fifty persons are working in the unit. The unit finally settled its dues under OTS.

Asset Reconstruction Companies (ARC) and Functions

All transactions of securitisation, reconstruction and creation of security interest shall be registered with a Central Registry maintained with the Union Government. Within 30 days of securitising the asset, details of securities have to be filed with the central registry by paying the required fees.

RBI has issued guidelines in 2003 on the form of offer and details to be incorporated therein. The most usual form is the Security Receipt (SR) and an agreement with the originator to continue to service the assets of the securitisation. It can also take the form of a debenture at no less than 1.5 per cent above the bank rate. The ARC should notify a separate scheme for each financial asset acquired or proposed to be acquired. Scheme-wise the account shall be maintained. Although security receipt is a tradable receipt among the investor institutions there is no such evidence thus far.

Realisation of the asset is held and applied towards redemption of the investments as assured while issuing the security receipt. It acts like a trustee managing the assets and does not become the owner of the assets. ARC can sell or lease out the assets for realising the value of the assets. The recovered amount of the discounted price of the asset will be shared between the bank and ARC in 85:15 ratio. For example, if a loan of Rs 100 lakh is sold for Rs 60 lakh to the ARC and the ARC realises only Rs 50 lakh on sale or the entire armoury at its command, the bank will get Rs 42.50 lakh for fully wiping out the account from its books. Once the asset is sold off, it ceases to be NPA in its books.

If the intention of the bank were to recover as much as possible from the stressed asset, it would be wise to explore OTS as first option within the RBI guidelines. We have noticed that in no more than 5 per cent of cases has this option been exercised as the bonafides in OTS transaction is suspect. It would be prudent on the part of the RBI to ensure that the OTS option is exhausted before going for securitisation and sale of the asset.

The other option is to seek the Banking Ombudsman's intervention as Arbitrator to settle the distressed asset closure in cases where either the borrower or the bank has reason to believe that a mutually agreed price of the loan would be a better option than proceeding against the asset under SARFAESI Act.

Banks can proactively solve the NPAs in MSE sector if they keep their eyes and ears open. Impact of sectorial failures caused by economic downturn both within and outside the country is available in the periodic assessments of various organisations indicated above. Similarly, they are also aware of which of the large and medium enterprises are postponing payments to their vendors, viz., MSEs. In both the instances banks can proactively provide succour to the weaklings in the industry through the periodic rescheduling of repayments when they will continue to be treated as standard assets if they are able to pay up the interest obligation. This is not to be treated as revival effort but a survival effort.

In all other cases, revival as per the RBI directives can be done in good time. It is imprudent for a bank to wait for the account to become

NPA to attempt revival process as is sometimes, some banks are choosing to do. Alert banks can significantly reduce the NPAs of MSEs.

FINANCE FIRMED THE LINK

Link Fasteners and Fabricators

The unit is a proprietary concern with P. Susheela Raju, wife of Chandrashekhar Raju, as proprietrix, engaged in the manufacture of industrial fasteners, bolts and nuts. The unit had a turnover of Rs 20 lakh in 2000 and moved over to Rs 35 lakh in 2003 and has been working on a very low profit margin. It has been enjoying a cash credit limit of Rs 8 lakh and a bill limit of Rs 9.54 lakh with the bank (PSB). The unit was on the brink of slippage in terms of its obligations when it secured a work order worth Rs 43 lakh. At this juncture, the bank came up with SME plus product and granted a limit of Rs 1.54 lakh, repayable in six weeks' time. The unit expressed its hope of honouring the commitment.

This is another case where the bank proactively prevented the unit from becoming NPA.

Contextually, ARCs never restructured MSMEs in India. They were just buying distressed assets at a price and selling off at a premium. Therefore, revival and restructure suffered at the systemic level. Further, the recently issued directive by RBI to restructure assets even while at the standard level – SMA (0-2) could end up the same way as erstwhile CDR and SDR mechanisms.

If the banks can follow the age-old proverb *A known devil is better than unknown angel*, there is a clear case for looking at the SARFAESI Act 2002 provisions under Section 13 that gave undue powers to the banks. Such powers blinded the banks to the option of reviving the revivable enterprises in good time. Therefore, the Act should be amended with the proviso that Section 13(C) can be invoked by banks only when an accredited institution like the Industrial Health Clinics, or Industry Associations having business advisory services window, certify that the MSE involved is non-revivable or when the bank categorically certifies that the unit is a wilful defaulter citing the provisions of the RBI circular on wilful default. The costs involved in the process should be met by the unit and the MSME Ministry, Government of India in equal proportion as a sick enterprise is incapable of meeting such expenditure.

Note

1. Yerram Raju B., "All About NPAs in MSMEs," *The Financial Express*, 24 March 2018.

12

Global Best Practices

'Businesses, even fairly small ones, will have to start their strategic thinking and planning with the world economy rather than with their own domestic economy.'– PETER DRUCKER[1]

Best practices need not be universal. They may or may not succeed when the country's overall ecosystem is incongruous with the country where it succeeded. These indicative best practices should be tested for stakeholder acceptance and regulatory regime of the country. It also depends upon the areas we are looking into: e.g., finance; administration and facilitation. The countries chosen for discussion are the US, Malaysia, European Union, Israel and Lebanon, South Africa, Taiwan, Germany, and the UK.

Keeping the job creation potential of SMEs in view, how can we create 100 million SMEs to spawn growth?

In the Finance Space:

- ❖ Culture of dependency has to change to self-reliance mechanism;
- ❖ Public sector and government departments have to pay within 15 days of receipt of goods invoiced and despatched.
- ❖ HR systems as of today are not able to attract smart people and retain them.

- In a knowledge-based economy, reskilling and upskilling strategies have to evolve within the capabilities of the SMEs: how to support the environment for such ecosystem, what should the governments do?
- Clusters: While there are 1500 clusters, identify those that have agglomeration effect on growth and create conditions for replication.

1. The US

The US example has many lessons:

- Small Business Act extends protection to the SMEs significantly
- States work with 68 District Offices
- District Offices work with Commerce departments
- Develop private sector capacity
- Co-funding from Small Business Development Centers
- 10,000 Senior Executives train the SMEs
- Regulatory Impact Assessment Studies are regularly undertaken and feedback provided to the Federal Authority
- Distribution and over-concentration is studied and corrected

Banks like scalable and efficient model for financing while several enterprises need patient capital. The model adopted is that the enterprise is funded by way of equity instead of debt with equity realisation linked to cash flow projections spread over 10 years. Once the SME realises the full potential this firm moves to the mezzanine or debt capital to the extent required to grow at the speed assessed.

Three levels of assessment persist:

- Self-assessment that does not involve any costs;
- In-house Micro Comprehensive Rating Enhancement;
- External Evaluation as decided by the HLTF.
- Online businesses are mostly owned by women. Home-grown champions

❖ **SME Master Plan** takes into consideration high impact programs. Home grown champions are showcased.

2. Malaysia

Malaysia established SME Corporation as a statutory body under the SME Corp. Act 539 of 2009. An empowered SME Agency is the central co-ordinating authority for SME development. Its roles and responsibilities include direction for comprehensive development of SMEs across all sectors. It formulates broad policies and strategies and overseas coordination and ensures effectiveness in policy implementation.

Philosophy: If the SMEs cannot serve themselves, they can't serve others.

The PM chairs the National SME Development Council where all the 17 state ministers dealing with SMEs are the members along with the Central Bank Governor and Chief Secretary. The Chief Secretary is the convenor. The Council meets once in a year. Differentiated policies exist for high growth firms and others. Twenty per cent or a little less constitute sectoral focus.

Programme Coordination and Working Committee (PCWC) with Secretaries of all the 17 Ministries with the Chief Secretary as Chairman reviews all the policies and discusses with the Industry Associations as also Private Sector Agencies. This meets at half-yearly intervals.

In addition, there is a High Level Task Force (HLTF) on SME development that monitors the implementation at the ground level all the policies. It ensures Business Advisory Support.

Thus, there is a three-level monitoring of the policy implementation.

In Malaysia, SMEs are defined in 2014 Act, 50 per cent of SMEs are in manufacturing while the rest are in services sector. SMEs contributed to 37 per cent of GDP as of March 2017.

National Macro performance is measured by GDP contribution, exports and employment.

SME Central Incentive System is a back-ended support based on programme performance. SME Integrated Action Plan is prepared annually by the HLTF.

Finance is provided to select companies from the SME development fund.

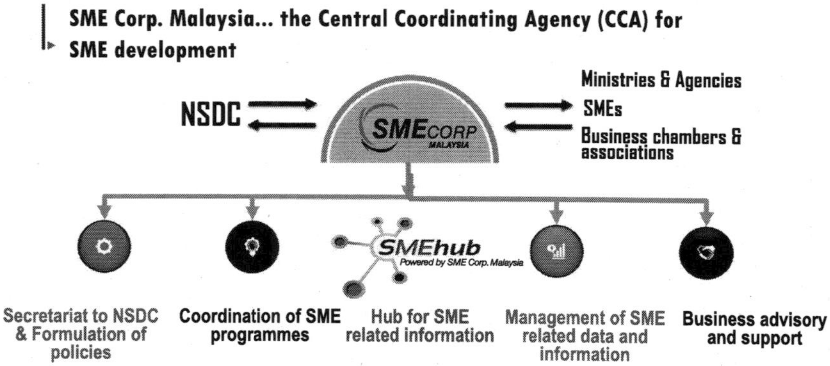

Source: SME Corporation, Government of Malaysia – presentation made at the India SME Road Map Workshop at Goa on 3 December 2018.

It operates on a result based approach through effective monitoring and evaluation periodically.

3. European Union, Israel and Lebanon (Middle East)

In both European Union and Israel, innovation, knowledge and skill development and dealing with venture capital markets have surfaced as success points. They do not have Manuals to provide a direction and support the SMEs.

Lebanon has job creation as the criteria for classifying an SME. It speaks dynamically of financing SMEs, thereby providing scope for graduation from small to medium through equity participation in firm development.

4. South Africa

South Africa emphasises on Start-ups and Social Capital. In this country, after school curriculum, training is provided in digitisation mandatorily two years after school education for women and three years for men.

Mentoring and counselling for SMEs; capturing value added per person employed by the SMEs, individual and group training in SMEs, regional development are the areas of specific attention of the government. Since the size of the nation is small, 90 per cent of the SMEs are engaged in producing for global markets where quality and quantity of production have a significant role to play apart from the EXIM Policy to stay ahead in global markets.

5. Germany

The German economy stands on the four pillars of Mittelstand, Vocational training, Trade Fairs and Industry Associations. It defines *Mittelstand (SMEs) in terms of 500 employees and 59 million Euros Turnover.* All the enterprises fall under the corporate segment—small to medium, in electrical, engineering and often manufacturing capital equipment family-owned enterprise space. They go by focused strategy and are deep instead of wide. Predictability of cycle and proximity of customers drive the enterprises to growth. As many as 1,300 world market leaders with niche products are the Mittelstand constituency. All debtors to SMEs in Germany by statute have to pay within 30 days of the due date and additional 15 days attract penalty of 2 per cent payable automatically. Failure attracts higher penalties and de-recognition of enterprise for further trade. As many as 52 per cent of school-going students are enrolled for vocational training. By the time they finish school study, they will be ripe for either employment or enterprise or further education. SMEs encourage employee participation in evolving and implementing business development strategies. Still, the following challenges remain:

- Getting skilled employees;
- Brand image;
- Increasing costs of operation;
- Slow in globalising – management, language;
- Suspicious in localisation – technology, skills, IP;
- Need support in Industries 4.0 and New Technologies;
- Female participation.

6. Poland

Poland has involved universities in rating the enterprises based on evidence of performance. Star 3 and above will receive grant support. Innovation and products are the drivers of growth.

7. Taiwan SMEs – Government initiatives[2]

Start-up & Incubation

The Government of Taiwan endeavours to build a platform for enterprise start-up and incubation through the following programmes:

a. Establishing a support mechanism for starting enterprises

Assisting individuals with fulfilling their dreams of starting enterprises, it is providing information and consultative services on starting an enterprise and creating a knowledge database website for start-up enterprises; is establishing schools that teach entrepreneurship and fulfilling the dream of starting a business; is giving awards to new enterprises, and is providing would-be entrepreneurs with systematic, phased assistance to boost the success rate and encourage individuals to start SMEs and facilitate economic growth.

b. Enhancing the Function of Incubation Service

1. By consolidating the advantages in terms of the specialties and resources of the incubation centres of universities, legal persons, governments and private enterprises, it provides incubation services ranging from creativity and innovation to starting enterprises, establishing a comprehensive incubation system for individuals intending to start their own enterprises, and satisfying enterprises' needs to start new enterprises and innovate.
2. Through the establishment of a development mechanism for incubation centres, it encourages enterprises to innovate and release R&D capacity, promote exchange and cooperation between incubation centres, enforce the performance evaluation system for incubation centres, raise incubation centres' service

quality, expand training centres' assistance capacity, and create a quality environment favourable for SMEs to innovate and develop.

c. Strengthening SME human resource development

1. Engaging in small and medium enterprise management and consultant seed personnel training work to raise business owners and employee management abilities. It selects and dispatches science and technology R&D personnel overseas for research and observation. It acquires R&D technology to enhance small and medium enterprise global competitiveness.
2. Setting up northern, central and southern small and medium enterprise research and training centres that combine the resources of schools and training institutes.

   It mutually promotes the lifelong learning passport and encourages the lifelong learning of enterprise employees. It implements regional personnel training requirement surveys to hold management courses that meet the needs of local industries. It has established a small and medium enterprise Internet university to promote online learning courses and continually train the personnel needed by SMEs.

d. Participation in international activities and the cultivation of international SME talent

Working earnestly to cultivate internationally-oriented talents to meet the emerging needs of this new era of globalisation.

Through the international economic and trade organisations such as the WTO, OECD and APEC as well as various occasions of bilateral cooperation, the Administration promotes work with SMEs from other nations to further participate in international economic and trade events and to expand develop international business opportunities.

Management

SMEs are the foundations of Taiwan's economic development. With their great flexibility, they have created economic miracles. In recent years, due to the rapid domestic and foreign politico-economic changes, SME operations become difficult. In light of this, they are in charge of hosting meetings on the status of 11 SME assistance systems. Each year, a national SME development conference is held to formulate SME development policies. Each quarter, an SME assistance system working meeting is held to coordinate and consolidate the assistance functions of the assistance systems. Furthermore, the mission is carried out through the following programmes and initiatives:

a. Strengthening management quality and promoting upgrading and transformation

To assist SMEs in making good use of government resources.

Business opportunities for SMEs are promoted through the successful upgrading and transformation of SMEs and announcements of new industries and products. The Administration also engages in enforcing diagnosis and guidance on the running and management of SMEs, coordinating and planning the establishment of corporate organisational management systems in order to improve corporate operating health, promoting the establishment of a technical exchange mechanism, and in accelerating the upgrading and transformation of SMEs.

b. Helping SMEs to secure business opportunities through government procurement

1. Through the service centre to help SMEs to participate in government procurement, provide information on government purchasing legislation, and help SMEs to overcome the problems that they experience when trying to participate in government procurement.
2. Published Questions and Answers on SME Participation in Government Procurement; have established a procurement website for SMEs, and collect data on the percentage of government procurement accounted for by SMEs. They are thus helping to create an environment in which SMEs can participate in government procurement on a level playing field.

c. Upgrading the function of the SME service network

They integrate the resources of local government agencies' SME service centres, local chambers of commerce and other relevant agencies, honorary SME guidance personnel (enterprise service volunteers) and are building up a comprehensive SME service mechanism, so as to be able to provide SMEs with information and resources, and thereby respond effectively to SMEs' problems and needs.

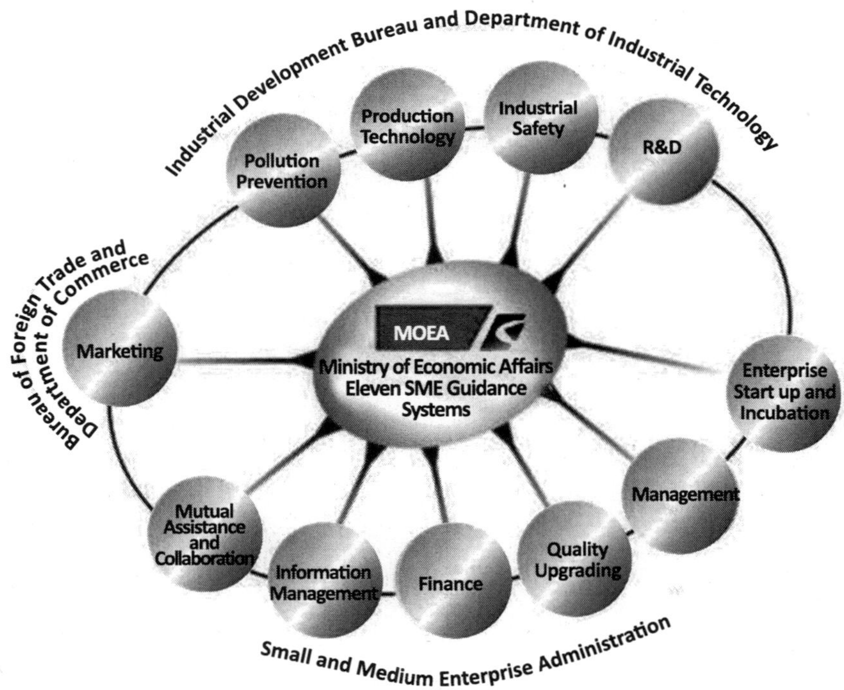

Note:

Ministry of Economic Affairs' Eleven SME Guidance Systems include:

1. Management
2. Quality Upgrading
3. Finance
4. Information Management

5. Mutual Assistance and Collaboration
6. Enterprise Start up and Incubation
7. Marketing
8. Pollution Prevention
9. Production Technology
10. Industrial Safety
11. R&D

The SMEA is responsible for 1–6, the Bureau of Foreign Trade and the Department of Commerce are responsible for 7, and the Industrial Development Bureau and the Department of Industrial Technology are responsible for 8–11.

Quality Upgradation

In order to assist SMEs in implementing quality upgrade and strengthening their quality management capabilities, the Administration has been providing quality improvement guidance for industry clusters in individual industries, helping them to conform to international environmental regulations, and providing SMEs with the guidance they need to secure TS 16949, ISO 14001 and QC 080000 certification, which in turn will help them to secure contracts from leading international companies.

They have been working to promote quality awareness, and to encourage the adoption of new quality management methods and concepts. They provide SMEs with guidance relating to Total Quality Management (TQM), 5S, Six Sigma, process management, restructuring and other quality management related concepts and issues, with the aim of raising quality levels in the SME sector.

Finance Assistance

In order to build up communication channels between SMEs and the SME Credit Guarantee Fund or the financial institutions and assist the SMEs to achieve perpetual development. The Administration carries out its mission through the following programmes and services:

1. Establishing One-stop Service Centre and providing emergency aid to SMEs. With the coordination and assistance from professionals, SMEs are immediately responded to. This centre also promotes the financing diagnostic assistance programmes to assist SMEs in obtaining operating funds.
2. Promoting a Financing Service Team Project corps for SMEs, with consultants providing immediate diagnostic assistance locally. Consultative services on finance, accounting, financing issues and operating plans are provided to SMEs before their applications to banks for loans are examined. The centre serves as a bridge of communication between SMEs and banks, assisting banks in understanding the SMEs' characteristics in order for SMEs to obtain financing without difficulty.
3. Being in charge of programmes for the promotion of financial knowledge, it is through the networks of industrial and commercial groups that the government's financial assistance measures are publicised. Training in financial management for the owners of SMEs is also strengthened. Help is provided to SMEs to enable them to correctly use the financial assistance resources provided by the government.
4. Strengthening the provision of diagnostic guidance to SMEs in the area of financing, thereby helping SMEs to improve their ability to secure loan credit guarantees.
5. Assisting SMEs with the establishment of financial management, internal control and accounting systems in an effort to enhance their management abilities.
6. Helping SMEs to secure loans, and works to expand the financing channel available to SMEs in order to solve the problems that they experience in securing working capital.
7. Providing with various financing diagnostics and credit guarantees in an effort to lower their operating costs by combining the SME Credit Guarantee Fund and Small Business Integrated Assistance Centre funding resources.

Sources of Financing

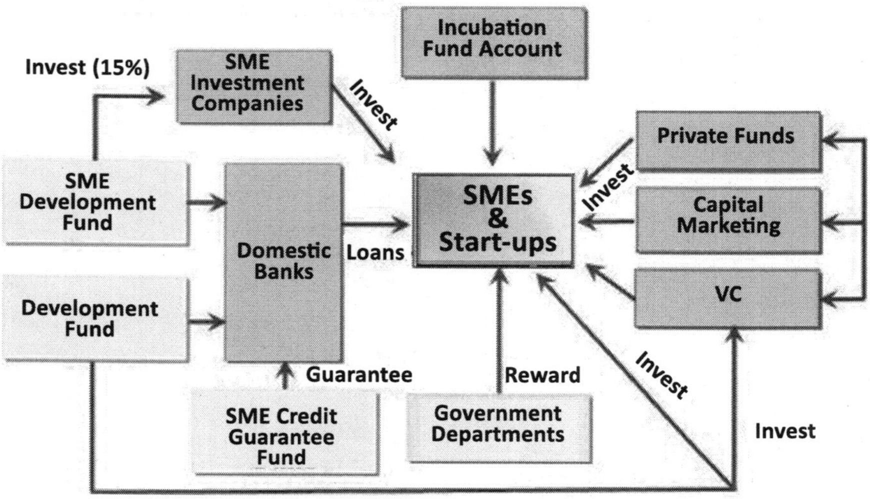

Note: The sources of financing for the SMEs and start-ups are including investing from private funds, incubation fund, SME Development Fund or capital markets, rewards from government departments, and loans from SME Credit Guarantee Fund.

Information Management

With over 1.2 million SMEs in Taiwan, SMEs are undoubtedly the key drivers to Taiwan's economic boom in recent decades. From a macroscopic point of view, SMEs encompass 98 per cent of all Taiwanese enterprises, and are spread across multiple sectors. However, the degree of information and communications technology (ICT) adoption varies greatly from company to company. In an effort to help transform, modernise, and encourage innovation for SMEs, it is imperative to introduce ICT to SMEs in an effort to expand their market opportunities and enhance their competitiveness. To achieve this goal, they are provided a number of services, including implementation of basic infrastructures, ICT applications, e-Commerce, and utilising ICT to encourage and facilitate innovation in businesses, to name a few.

Mutual Assistance & Collaboration

The purpose of Mutual Assistance and Collaboration guidance is to promote of mutual assistance between enterprises. It seeks to expand the promotion and collaboration between SMEs, so that SMEs can share operational resources and work together to develop new products and new technologies. This will help SMEs to develop new market opportunities.

Furthermore, the Administration is making use of existing industry cluster resources to provide guidance for the establishment of sound enterprise networks, strengthen collaboration between companies in the same cluster, and upgrade overall management capability.

They carry out this mission through the following programmes and services:

1. Arrange for the enterprises with the intention of mutual assistance to join the mutual assistance guidance system.
2. Instruct the cooperation and exchange association: Assist in the formulation of the regulations for the cooperation and exchange association; assist in the organisation of activities for the association, build up consensus with the committee; help them propose feasible collaborative ideas; guide them with the selection of the topic for their cooperation; and then conduct feasibility studies.
3. Instruct the actual collaboration projects:

   Help the actual collaboration projects formulate the regulations for joint development, organise the cooperative businesses, formulate marketing and production for cooperative businesses, and obtain the resources available in the outside environment.

   Through these comprehensive ICT guidance services, the Administration aims to e-Enable Taiwan's SMEs and help achieve their dreams of modernisation and embrace the challenges brought forth by the digital economy.

   Integrating resources from all sectors around Taiwan, the Administration categorizes the e-Business Enabling process into various stages, including implementation of basic infrastructures, ICT applications, and e-Commerce.

Projects & Services	Framework	Scope of Projects
SME International Web Marketing Project	e-Commerce	International Online Sales
SME e-Business Innovation Service	e-Application	e-Operations In-depth Application
The SME e-care Programme	e-Infrastructure	Communications

Regulations Assistance

To create a healthy environment for the development of SMEs, the following programmes and initiatives have been launched:

a. Assertion of SMEs' rights by regulatory adjustment

1. Promoting the establishment of an analytical mechanism to coordinate regulations governing SMEs in order for government at all levels to evaluate the scale and characteristics of SMEs when drawing up or revising regulations governing SMEs, which makes it easier for SMEs to abide by the regulations and promotes innovation, growth and the development of SMEs.
2. Promoting a "System of Honorary Consultative Attorneys for SMEs" project, by establishing a well-rounded consultative service on regulations to provide a consultative channel on regulations and reinforce information services for regulations on corporate operations, conducting seminars on issues regarding regulations governing SMEs, and for expanding the scope of service of the regulations governing firms' operations in an effort to effectively enhance the SMEs' ability to respond to regulations and strengthen the SMEs' competitiveness.
3. Conducting the propaganda on SMEs regulations and laws to collect the relative questions and reply, coordinate with correlative government agencies. In case response to such questions needs adjustment or amendment to laws or administrative regulations, the mechanism, "SMEs Development Operation Assembly in Legislation Yuan" will be convened to coordinate and review. By the

implementation of above measures, the SMEA assures the healthy laws environment for the development of SMEs.

b. Research on and analysis of the SMEs' business environment

1. They collect and analyze statistics relating to the SMEs' operating activities. This enables us to keep its finger on the pulse of SME operations. Every year, they publish a White Paper on Small and Medium Enterprises in Taiwan, which is a valuable reference for both SMEs and other government agencies.
2. They handle the statistics, surveys and studies related to SMEs, and undertake the evaluation and analysis of policy issues related to SME development. Through a policy review procedure, they reach a consensus to serve as reference for related government agencies in the preparation of SME policies, laws and regulations.

c. Promoting comprehensive planning matters

1. Regarding changes at home or in the overseas economic and trade environment, economic development strategies and measures are planned for SMEs and their needs. This office is in charge of the Committee for the Review of SME Policy and the Committee for Consultation on the Industry Development of SMEs in order to establish a good environment for the development of SMEs.

The office compiles a Collection of Success Stories of SMEs, describing the development of enterprises, and analyzing the key factors to their success. Criteria for corporate success are forwarded to SMEs for their reference. SMEs are urged to provide manpower to assist in the implementation of programs, and they are encouraged to employ more of the unemployed in order to raise labor quality and boost employment.

Local Culture Industries

In order to help local culture industries to develop value-added products and services based on their 'uniqueness'. They launched a series of guidance projects to stimulate the growth of local cultural enterprises. Through providing these projects and services for local feature industries and small community enterprises and assisting businesses in using existing resources with leisure and tourism events to develop and promote business features. It is also promoting business-type changes to raise the added value of products. It is enthusiastically developing a creative local feature industry and small community enterprises, and is integrating all local resources to advance local feature industry development.

Besides, we also encourage the development of innovative local SMEs in rural areas in order to integrate industries with local characteristics, and thereby improve local industries and encourage innovation and industrial development. It is collaborating with other government agencies on reconstruction work in areas where there have been natural disasters. It is helping SMEs to be productively involved in restoring the local economy to health.

Notes

1. Managing in Turbulent Environments in "Managing in Turbulent Times" (1980), Harper & Row Publishers Inc., p. 178
2. http://www.moeasmea.gov.tw/ct.asp?xItem=2568&CtNode=327&mp=2

References

Raju, B. Yerram:

a. "Giving a big push to small, medium enterprises." BusinessLine, 6 October 2016. https://www.thehindubusinessline.com/specials/giving-a-big-push-to-small-medium-enterprises/article9189241.ece
b. "MSMEs Become the Buzz Word Again." Telangana Today, 22 December 2018. https://telanganatoday.com/making-msmes-buzz-again
c. "Pain points for the MSME sector." *BusinessLine*, 26 December 2018. https://www.thehindubusinessline.com/opinion/pain-points-for-the-msme-sector/article25835822.ece
d. "MSME Amendment Bill will destroy the sector." *Moneylife News & Views*, 8 June 2016. https://www.moneylife.in/article/msme-amendment-bill-will-destroy-the-sector/47160.html

e. "Mending MSME Lending." *Financial Express*, 9 February 2009.

f. "NPAs of MSEs need alert Banking." *KNN India*, 18 July 2017. https://knnindia.co.in/news/newsdetails/msme/npas-of-mses-need-alert-banking

g. "GoI Draft Industrial Policy 2017." *KNNIndia*, 16 September 2017.

h. "TIHCL Inching Forward." *Telangana Today*, 19 March 2018.

i. "Reclassifying MSMEs: The turnover criterion will cause confusion." *BusinessLine*, 31 July 2018. https://www.thehindubusinessline.com/opinion/reclassifying-msmes/article24565351.ece

j. "Bet big on MSMEs in Telangana." *Telangana Today, 6 September 2018.* https://telanganatoday.com/bet-big-on-msmes-in-telangana

13

Technology and MSMEs

The role of technology in MSMEs, though never underestimated, requires much more than what has so far been done. This is for two reasons:

1. Indian entrepreneurs are overconfident of their innovative capabilities. They tend to import low cost technology with a view to modifying it to produce a superior product competitively. It is not uncommon to see that many a time obsolete technology is imported. In the process, the entrepreneur fails to realise upfront that he is losing out product competitiveness as his counterpart produces similar goods with superior technology at a better price.
2. The latest technologies carry with them IPR that are costly. In addition to these, the counselling or mentoring on new technologies does not also take place either from the DIC officials who are themselves behind by a generation. Linkages between the scientific and technology research organisations and industry are also not strong despite government efforts.

An environment for building competitiveness among SMEs through induction of emerging technologies needs to be part of the industrial ecosystem.

To unleash the full power of technology as a driver of revenue growth, firms must overcome the silos that prevent them from harnessing insights across the enterprise.

Leaders deploy a variety of technologies in service of customers and in bridging the gaps across departmental divides that stymie many transformations. Challenges exist and must be surmounted, but improvements to customer acquisition, retention, and revenue growth suggest that a transformation strategy is needed for survival.

It is desirable to set up an MSME–Technology Mission comprising of representatives of science and technology related ministries, leading national institutes, research bodies, industry representatives and other stakeholders on the lines of Government of Telangana's Research and Innovation Circle of Hyderabad (RICH). RICH captures the latest adaptable technologies from both within and outside the country and takes them to commercial levels with proper networking with industry. However, the reach to the MSMEs even by such an institution needs improvement. Technology Mission can explore emerging technologies suitable for MSMEs, arrange for dissemination of these technologies, facilitate transfer of technology, encourage R&D activities, and create technology incubator facilities for technologies suitable for MSMEs. Overall, this Mission would act as single window source for technologies appropriate for MSMEs. Costs of transmission, IPR costs, commercialisation of innovation must be supported by the proposed Technology and Innovation Fund, with initial contribution from Government of India, which would be open for contributions from state governments, industry bodies and voluntary contributions from the academic and research institutions, alumni associations, both within and outside the country. This can be operated on the lines of National Innovation Foundation, an autonomous body under the Department of Science & Technology.

The Technology Information Forecasting & Assessment Council (TIFAC) – MSME programme provides a platform for facilitating interactions of MSMEs with academia/R&D and Technical Institutions. The emphasis should be on providing technical support to the MSMEs by leveraging the knowledge base of TIFAC, academic institutions,

R&D centres of CSIR and Technical Institutes. The approach starts with technology mapping and comprehensive assessment of technology needs with specific focus on technology status, identification of gaps, and designing a technology intervention plan.

The Ministry of MSME should revamp its grassroots organisations to enable them identify emerging technologies and support transfer of technology. DICs should be rechristened as District Enterprise Development Centres and reoriented to be the extension arm of Technology Mission and TIFAC but without the powers to distribute incentives.

The industry associations should also be roped in to take the efforts of technology upgradation to maturity levels. CII has established an SME Technology Facilitation Centre to provide latest technology support to SMEs in India. It is operating as a one-stop shop, summating different upgraded and latest technologies from multiple technology partners and aims to enhance access to technology for Indian SMEs; and create technical literacy amongst them. The CII Centre also provides an opportunity to its technology partners to expand their market and reach out to SMEs spread throughout the country.

Every innovation carries with it some cost for commercialisation. It also requires branding or co-branding to go the commercial way. The cost of such process cannot be expected to be absorbed by a loan. Hence, it is advisable to fund the process of commercialisation after proper evaluation by the government.

At the other end of the spectrum, MSMEs need to move to digitise their entire operations that include their setting up ERP platforms. If the banks and financial institutions lost trust in the MSMEs, it was due to their non-compliance of terms and sanction of credit limits and absence of frequent communication between them. This compliance risk can be mitigated successfully through ERP solutions and consent-based architecture for sharing the essential data required for monitoring credit utilisation. Digital Accountants Training Programme initiated by the TIHCL in coordination with the CITD would help converting the unorganised to organised sector over a short period.

The guidepost should address the following aspects:

Product development; Integrating into global/ regional/local value chains

- ❖ Does every link add value to the chain? How to build cost effective checks and balances?
- ❖ Digital Business Data – Leveraging for Enhancing Capacities;
- ❖ Establishing operational and financial benchmarking standards.

Assessing firm-level performance:

- ❖ Zero Effect, Zero Defect and GeM of GoI – Awareness should be followed by monitoring and impact assessment studies;
- ❖ Every Scheme of the Government should be monitored and evaluated for results once in a year structurally and those with marginal contribution should be taken off the window of support;
- ❖ Building Credit Information through Electronic Invoicing – GeM and GST facilitate but need greater traction. All the state governments and state PSUs should fall in line.

ITES SMEs have reached a level of maturity in software but a long way to go in hardware or manufacturing SMEs in IT industry. It is highly desirable for the government to distinguish services from manufacturing in IT so that we do not indulge in the luxury of frequent extolling of software technologies as the be-all and end-all of technology transformation.

We have already created a niche for ourselves in software and Apps. But this will not sustain unless we move our focus to the manufacturing SMEs. The entire start-up ecosystem today is like the dotcom of yester-years. Angel investors and VCs or Private Equity providers are hardly noticed in the investing sphere of manufacturing technologies. States like Karnataka, AP, Telangana and Haryana have put in an excellent ecosystem for the start-ups through Hub and Spoke models and technology is basically knowledge and innovation driven. Hence, the policy framework shall provide the needed wherewithal to the upcoming generation from the technical institutions to turn to enterprise promotion and not wage-driven. We are creating more computer coolies than technology innovators.

We have made significant strides in computer Hardware and Software in the finance space with the setting up of National Payments and Settlement systems, Trade Credit Exchange instruments and mobile technologies. Financial sector and Technology firms are going in sync with each other. The most risky part of the game is in cyber risks that are posing very big challenge. This needs to be addressed adequately and appropriately lest the losses cannot be recuperated. Banks jump at funding Apps and software but drag their feet for funding manufacturing MSEs who want to adopt latest technologies.

IT majors like HP are big enablers for efficiency. HP should move to customer-friendly technologies. Their efficient printers are cost intensive with the software price eating the gains in hardware. Outdated technologies should be moved out of the market by a re-purchase or junk channel once there is change in the technology. Innovation lies in adoption commercially. Commercial uptake is linked to pricing and the incentives built around it. Markets are becoming increasingly sensitive to technology adoption and pricing. Franchisees and Service providers need periodical refreshers by the HP.

Companies like HP have major focus towards SMB segment and they innovate a great deal to meet the varied demands of the sector but their performance needs to be watched with care.

Focus on Digital India, e-governance, start-up India can be still in the comfort zone if the governments (Union and state) would give up their love for big IT firms when they call for tenders. The tender specs should be oriented towards SMEs more. The turnover stipulation is hostile to SMEs. If they would like to join a big IT firm it has its costs. Big IT firms can encourage SMEs to be their partners; they can co-brand with the SMEs; they can build competencies that are germane to vertical growth.

Data security should go with data integrity. Checks and cross-checks in data generation and output are not able to ensure data integrity. Without data integrity big data and DAAS will be a disaster as it is already happening in banking, insurance, telecom, pharma, etc. There should be built-in incentives for data integrity; counselling, mentoring and training should be given by those who would have shown the way for establishing reliable data systems across industries.

Finance is critical for growth of any industry. Banks and FIs want proof of concept before funding for upgrading the technologies. This proof can come from funding by angel investors and VCs. Although SIDBI operates Technology Upgradation Fund its performance over the years in the SME sector leaves much to be desired. It is perhaps desirable that we build some accountability for performance under prescribed timelines for the corporate established through statute, to the Parliament at the first session following the budget session each year. Regulatory institutions should own up responsibility and ensure that the guidelines for implementing the policies released by the government are followed in word and spirit.

14

Exit Policy for the MSEs

The high-risk, high-return nature of many MSE ventures, coupled with a high debt/capital ratio, exposes them to business cycle fluctuation, especially because they lack the cushion capital to respond to bank requirements during economic downturns. The National Equity Fund schemes, common in the region and in operation in India for the last 20 years, have very poor pick-up rates, as access procedures are too complex for the average entrepreneurs. Of particular interest are Mutual Guarantee programmes with MSE Associations promoting group borrowing and leveraging on public guarantee funds for wider coverage.

Firms continue to finance their requirements under a pecking-order framework: rather, in a hierarchical fashion: first, by using their internally available savings, family contributions followed by debt and finally, by equity. Venture Capitals come near only those enterprises that have established marketing channels and proven delivery systems with an annual yield rate of >30 per cent because they also seek exit routes.

Institutional bankruptcy and individual insolvency provisions should be part of such exercise whereby the state that has played a dominant role in promoting the sector with subsidies and grants should not lose out and at the same time the entrepreneur with limited resources and a larger canvas to live honourably would have that option at least cost. Everybody and anybody can have a retirement but not the entrepreneur.

Therefore, the policy should involve provisions for:

1. Mid-course corrections for an entrepreneur to exit
2. Flexibility to shift from liquidation to rehabilitation and vice versa
3. No special provisions for claims for the public sector organisations or government agencies vis-à-vis other creditors
4. Legal process should encourage informal settlement.
5. No creditor should be in a position to institute criminal cases against mere defaults.
6. While there are some insurance mechanisms, they were all pre-reform in the insurance sector. These would also require a review and reformulation to help both the entrepreneur and the labour.

Development of MSEs is a state subject and the state is well within its rights to formulate suitable policies in the interest of the healthy growth of the sector and also, if necessary, frame suitable laws in that direction.

EXIT POLICY FORMULATIONS FOR CONSIDERATION

Category 1- Owner Entrepreneurs

All the proprietary enterprises shall mention in their application for registration nomination particulars: That is, the proprietors shall nominate the details of person(s) in whose favour the assets and liabilities of the enterprise shall get transferred either after them or should they choose to wind up their enterprise.

In case of existing entrepreneurs such nomination, which is irrevocable, shall be filed by means of an affidavit on Rs 100 stamp paper, giving the nomination details.

The nomination details should contain the following particulars, with two passport size photographs:

1. Name of the person:
2. Age:
3. Permanent Address:

(Any change in the address shall be intimated with the copy of the recorded change to be acknowledged by the General Manager, District Industries Centre)

4. Relationship of the nominee with the Applicant

Signature:

Place:

In case of electronic form, the digital signature of the applicant shall be affixed. The digital signature can be obtained from the approved institutions like the Institute for Development Research in Banking Technology, Hyderabad.

A doubt has been expressed that such nominee may accept the assets and not liabilities. In order to resolve this, it is proposed that the acceptance of the nominee may also be obtained up front by way of an irrevocable undertaking with two independent witnesses.

Since minor children, if nominated, may also raise objection to such nomination on attaining majority, nomination of minor does not fall under the eligible category of nominees.

Route for Exit for this category shall be the last option:

> An opportunity should be provided to improve the skills of the entrepreneurs.

Separate mechanism to be set up with apex body to deal the problems of such entrepreneurs:

> The entrepreneur should first approach the Body – This Body we designate as the Commission for settlement of stressed assets (CSSA). The CSAA would therefore deal with the problem of exit of entrepreneur and enterprise on two separate sets of criteria.

Identification of the problem of the entrepreneur:

> Provide necessary expertise, advice, guidance and assistance so that the entrepreneur can acquire necessary skills to run the enterprise profitably and by giving training.

Last resort: takeover of the assets and liabilities by the Government and pave the way for the exit of the entrepreneur by providing reasonable compensation.

The state government can conduct bids for selling the enterprise and the bid price can be recovered from the proceeds of sale. DICs can be the nodal agencies.

Category 2

When strategising about the transition, it is important to separate 'management' from 'ownership'.

Asset Reconstruction Companies registered with the RBI shall, on the recommendation of the State CSSA, arrange for transparent pricing and transfer of assets at such price unto itself at such terms as are negotiated with the state-level committee for which the State Commissioner would be the Member Secretary. The state exchequer would be entitled for fees not less than 0.5 per cent of the asset value or Rs 10,000, whichever is high. Fifty per cent of such fees should be paid on acceptance of the proposal by the CSSA.

Category 3- Partnership Firms

Partnership firms are advised to migrate to Limited Liability Partnership form of business organisation under the LLP Act, 2008 and this form has built in route for exit of partners. Unfortunately, LLPs are difficult to form for manufacturing firms as the RBI and Banks do not recognise these structures as eligible for credit support.

Amendment to the Arbitration Act:

> Those that continue as Partnerships under the Indian Partnership Act having disputes among the partners should first exhaust the option of arbitration under the Arbitration Act. Arbitration Act also needs amendment on the following lines: If the arbitrator is a retired judge at a particular level of the Court, say, Supreme Court or High Court, it cannot be contested in District Courts.
>
> In the case of partnership firms remaining as such but find it difficult to sell, the firm shall declare to wind up on such terms as would be decided by the state government's Tribunal for Settlement of Stressed Assets (TSSA). The firm shall sign

an irrevocable letter of authority to the TSSA for deciding on the value of assets and liabilities of the firm on the date of declaration of bankruptcy.

The tribunals should be given wide powers to settle issues like fraud or cheating, glaring financial irregularities like misuse of funds causing loss to the public exchequer and financial institutions and banks as rider on the activities of the entrepreneurs.

The TSSA may exercise the option of sale of enterprise to an Approved Asset Reconstruction Company for selling the Assets. The proceeds shall be distributed in the following priority after considering all the notified eligible exemptions:

1. Sovereign Creditor:
   (a) Excise and Customs Dues if any
   (b) Income Tax
   (c) Commercial taxes
   (d) Dues to the Electricity Department

2. Institutional Lenders: (a) Term Lending Institution (b) Working Capital Funding Institution.
3. Suppliers on the basis of First-In, First-Out (FIFO) and in such proportion as the creditors stand.

   Simple interest at 0.75 per cent or such low percentage per month on the outstanding creditors as on the date the firm declares to wind up till the date of sale to the ARC.

4. Fees due to the Commission for settlement of stressed assets.

   Residual amount, if any, shall be passed on to the firm's partners in equal proportion.

The partners of the firm, on such declaration, from that date of declaration shall be free to pursue such economic activities as would sustain them including seeking appointment to such assignments for which they would be considered eligible:

- Provided that none of them have been declared wilful defaulters by either the Government or the financing institutions;
- Provided also that none of them have faced any criminal charges or defalcations against them during the course of their running the enterprises.

Category 4- Women Entrepreneurs

It is imperative that all enterprises registered with the DIC/Commissioner and Director of Industries under Udyog Aadhar and submitting the Annual Returns prescribed under the MSMED Act 2006 shall alone be eligible for consideration under the Exit Scheme of the state government. (One may fail as an enterprise or entrepreneur but should have demonstrated his intention to abide by Law of the land.)

Insolvency and Bankruptcy Code:

> Bankruptcy Law 2016 though covers individuals to corporate entities it requires separate rules in regard to the micro and small enterprises as the large and medium enterprises would crowd out the micro and small enterprises.
>
> The Act does not also cover defaults of the state and Central government departments and most MSEs are vendors to the state projects. Several state governments also deny payments breaching the contracts, whether PPP or otherwise.
>
> Like free legal aid to certain classes of society, micro and small enterprises should be provided free legal and arbitration services at the cost of the government—state and Centre.

Credit-Development Synergies in a Federal System

While MSEs are essentially a regional subject with the predominant roles of the state governments, the financial resources available at the disposal of the state governments are often minimal. Since the beginning of the century, there has been an enhanced tendency towards the centralisation of MSE financing, through the hegemonic role of the Public sector banks and the SIDBI as the refinancing agency. The State Finance Corporations, which were key players in the pre-1990s, got seriously weakened. This would essentially mean two things: 1) poor credit off-take from the state level sources; and 2) A progressive distancing of all-India DFIs from their developmental activities. This has created a new space for NBFCs, which need to be examined in relation to their commitments to the overall development of the MSE sector. It is important to examine the role of SFCs, as also the relevance and constraints of the SFC Act (1951), in the special context of the national policy of decentralisation and empowerment of the state governments. Similarly, it is also important to critically examine the role of the co-operative banks in relation to MSE finance, as the co-operative credit system in the country shows a mixed picture differing from state to state. In the context of the general spirit of a massive broad basing of finance unleashed by MUDRA, the direction of policy needs to be the maximum exploitation of all state-level financial intermediaries. This may probably demand significant steps towards legislative reforms, especially the SFC Act and the Co-operatives Act, for which this policy encourages the state governments.

15

Green Shoots in Industrial Soil

A MODEL FOR REVIVING MICRO AND SMALL ENTERPRISES IN MANUFACTURING SECTOR

The industrial soil with dry patches and even some parched areas needed soil rejuvenation and watering for the green shoots to come up from the dried roots. Incipient sick and sick enterprises in the micro and small manufacturing space have been crying with none to care. While the Central Government is creating an eco-friendly environment correcting several pollutants that have crept into the system over the last few decades with positive interventions through digital technologies, states like Telangana are marching ahead with creating new strategies and new products in the MSME domain.

Telangana being a new state, the state government wanted to make a difference from the past and opened a new leaf with the starting of the Telangana Industrial Health Clinic Ltd. The concept has now caught up with the national policymakers.

Evolution

Policy drivers for resolution of sickness in MSMEs by both the Government and RBI and institutional mechanisms like the State-

Level Inter-institutional Committee and Empowerment Committee for MSMEs, unfortunately, did not yield the expected results for decades. In Telangana we noticed that even as at the middle of 2017, SLBC (State-Level Bankers' Committee) data revealed 10 per cent units in micro enterprises were revived with a measly average of Rs 4.5 lakh per unit. Medium enterprises can now file bankruptcy and seek resolution, thanks to the Insolvency and Bankruptcy Act. But the micro and small enterprises continue to sail in uncertain waters to revive. We veered round to the thinking of former RBI Governor Raghuram Rajan and Dy. Governor Deepak Mohanty that a separate institutional mechanism alone would be the best bet for resolution of stressed assets in MSEs.

After intense discussions with the Commissioner of Industries and Principal Secretary (I&C), the concept was presented in June 2016 to Telangana Minister for Industries K.T. Rama Rao who instantly piloted it. He announced in the Legislative Assembly that the state is going to establish an innovative institution to tackle endemic incipient sickness and sickness in the Micro and Small Enterprises in the manufacturing space.

Social Cost Benefit Analysis revealed huge gains on revival in terms of sustainable employment, higher happiness index, greater confidence for entrepreneurs that they can perform, higher revenues to the exchequer and healthy industrial climate fulfilling the UN's SDG 9th goal.

Process

A Committee of Secretaries was set up by the state government to examine the nature of such an institution. This Committee gave the green signal for setting up a public limited company under the Companies Act with the Telangana State Irrigation Development Corporation (TSIDC) anchoring it for formation. The work commenced with the think tank discussing the strategy, vision, mission, objectives, organisational structure, culture, investment model, governance and stakeholder management. It deliberated for nearly 200-man hours on the task.

The discussion on the problems noticeably centred around entrepreneurs' lack of knowledge of the environment in which they would operate, unidentified markets for their products, outdated technologies, deficiencies in products, packaging, processes, and lastly finance and lack of financial discipline. It has been recognised that they lack mentoring, counselling and guidance for resolving their problems at affordable costs with a sense of responsibility. They are misguided rather than guided properly. Inadequate and untimely delivery as also inappropriate financial products continues to be the reason for the alarming sickness in the sector.

Strategy

The strategy should offer solutions that would be acceptable to the financial institutions and suitable to the MSEs, rebuilding the lost trust between the financial institutions. The Telangana Industrial Health Clinic Ltd was set up to offer such solutions in the industrial ecosystem of the state that has unleashed the world acclaimed Industrial Policy.

There was broad consensus on the new institutional set-up that should have the support but minimal participation and least interference from the state or Union governments and should have ample scope to run professionally. Accordingly, it was decided to register the Telangana Industrial Health Clinic as a public limited company initially only to move it to the non-deposit taking, non-systemic NBFC platform by completing the registration formalities with the RBI. The RBI took about six months to accord its approval and the NBFC was set up on 2 April 2018.

The institution has to be a FinTech (Financial Technologies) company on a co-financing platform. The strategy is to rebuild the lost trust between the beleaguered enterprises and the primary lending institutions through comprehensive diagnosis with the involvement of experts in Finance, Marketing, and Technology and Strategic partnership. The institution should only supplement and not supplant the existing institutional setup. It would drive the entire initiative through transparency and autonomy. The Vision, Mission and Objectives were shared with the state government which agreed to lend the required support.

Vision

To build and develop sustainable entrepreneurial ecosystem dealing with challenges of manufacturing MSEs in Telangana

Mission

To guide, mentor and support manufacturing entrepreneurs to success

Values

Dharma – Righteousness; *Lok Sangraha* – Public Good; *Kaushalyam* – Skill and efficiency; *Vaividhyata* – Innovation; *Jignasa* – Learning

Organisational Structure

It was agreed to have a Board of Directors with the Chairman getting elected at every Board Meeting. It shall have a lean management with an MD & CEO at the top and three Vice Presidents of whom one would exclusively deal with technology. There would be one Admin Executive and six to eight Executives. There shall be no subordinate staff. This lean structure should continue until it goes to IPO at the end of the fourth or fifth year. The Board has set up a Recruitment Committee and Management Committee. Recruitment was ordained to be through Head Hunt for the MD & CEO and open recruitment for other positions.

A website was designed to reflect transparency, autonomy and knowledge as key drivers of the new institution. It was hosted by the state government. (www.tihcl.telangana.gov.in)

Process

Its uniqueness lies in transparent delivery mechanisms for all its promises with a sense of responsibility. The model involves working through a team of external experts who would be process consultants. They undertake diagnosis within five days of accepting the assignment after a visit to the concerned unit, discussions with the borrower(s) and their financing bank. The consultant is responsible for the solution offered and accepted by the primary lender. He would monitor the cash flows for 6–12 months depending on the need.

TIHCL proves its concept

Karimnagar district in Telangana has thrown up a few cases. An entrepreneur manufacturing unbranded detergent who received all accolades from the government found himself on the decks due to his market restricted only to the state government during 2008-14. Another from the same place engaged in manufacturing and innovative recycling of batteries for automobiles with market restricted to the state public transport undertaking that actually saved no less than Rs 35 lakh per month to the entity, became an NPA and sold off his property to settle debt under one-time settlement (OTS). A third entrepreneur, engaged in manufacturing paints at Jeedimetla IE in Hyderabad, similarly suffered in strategically positioning himself in the market.

In yet another case, a polymer unit in Palwancha town suffered due to partnership dispute and delayed release of state-announced incentives for the last three years. There were 23 entrepreneurs invited to establish handloom and power loom units in a textile park, but they suffered because of the promised infrastructure not materialising for years. All incentives due to them were released.

Forward and backward linkages were absent and they landed themselves in the NPA saga. We noticed that of the 52 NPAs or partially-closed units approaching us for resolution, 60 per cent were on sick bed due to non-financial problems—power failure or irregular power supply, heavy commercial tax dues in arrears and strategic management issues. And 38 per cent were due to delayed release of incentives, and 12 more units in steel and aluminium sector suffered due to high power costs and lost their competitiveness compared to other neighbouring states.

One of the large private banks indulged in lending to the MSMEs without due diligence and the limits were below Rs 10 lakh. They are shown in the NPA books although all of them qualify to be lent under the CGTMSE (Credit Guarantee Fund Trust for Micro and Small Enterprises). With regard to the other units with limits below Rs 50 lakh but above Rs 10 lakh, they did not even bother to conduct the Techno Economic Viability (TEV) study expected of them for revival for the past one year.

A PSB found a unit eligible for restructuring after the TEV study but imposed onerous conditions for restarting the unit. They were sold to the ARC even while the unit requested for OTS. Another PSB sanctioned term loan but did not release working capital as the unit failed to produce the market guarantee projected at the time of sanction. Term loan unserviced as a result is on the threshold of NPA.

Except 10 per cent, most of the problems of MSMEs required non-financial support—marketing strategy, product differentiation, process change, reprieve at the hands of the state government for waiver of power dues/interest, waiver or postponement of commercial tax arrears or financial literacy. Such support can hardly come from the banks who suffer from acute staff shortage at the credit monitoring platform. There are banks that have a myriad of SME loan products but sparsely delivered.

TIHCL enters into MoU with the banks concerned for this purpose and with the entrepreneur. The key components involve part-time accountant to manage and monitor the MIS and cash flows through ERP solutions set up with the unit mandatorily. Banks were initially reluctant to enter into MoUs with TIHCL. Industries Minister K.T. Rama Rao addressed the MSME subcommittee of SLBC and impressed on the bankers to kickstart the process and requested them to refer all cases where they were to issue notices under SARFAESI Act. Some rethinking from banks is yet to crystallise.

Capital Structure

Initial corpus of Rs 100 crore with contribution from the state government Rs 10 crore as equity; expected contribution of GoI as grant from out of the APSRA 2014 to the extent of Rs 50 crore (yet to materialise); MSEs – Rs 5 crore over five years; Banks and FIs: 50 per cent as equity; Associations – Rs 5 crore as equity over five years and the rest other stakeholders. TIHCL promises yield of 7 per cent with a lock-in period of two years. Structurally, the state government is expected to have minimum holding and the enterprise plans to go for initial public offering (IPO) at the end of five years.

Products

The products are designed around the co-financing model with the TIHCL having to shed the margin/catalytic component of 20 per cent of the identified gap in funding and insist on 5 per cent to come from the units. The margin fund carries interest at 5 per cent less than that charged by the Banks. The units have of course to pay the processing fees as decided by the Board. All payments will be online. Covenant risks are taken care of by proper execution of documents. Its document management system takes care of provisions acceptable to the primary lender and the units. Responsible and responsive diagnostics, consultancy, handholding and prompt attention are its strengths.

It has three verticals as of now: 1. Margin money up to Rs 25 lakh per MSE units for revival; 2. Rediscounting of bills drawn on either government or PSUs beyond the tenor; 3. Fresh funding in clusters for micro units within the 20 per cent cap; and up to Rs 50,000 grant support for TEV study.

Noticing that subsidies from the state government are delayed sometimes even beyond two years, TIHCL would be providing bridge finance initially at 12 per cent to the extent of 75 per cent of sanctioned subsidy at interest rate decided by the Board.

In most cases of revival, power to the unit would have been disconnected and required payment of arrears and reconnection charges that takes a good slice of the revival package. By an arrangement with the Distribution Company, TIHCL would release these arrears through a package decided by the state government so that the revival takes place as planned. An MoU between TIHCL and the Distribution Company would decide the modalities. The Distribution Company would release projected package at the beginning of the year.

Board

The First Board consisted of three Government Nominees; two official directors; four independent directors including a woman director; and one representative of the Association.

Management

A retired General Manager (FIDD), RBI and Faculty of IDRBT as MD and CEO; COO—a retired GM of SBI with over 36 years of experience in lending and treasury management, among others; Two Vice Presidents—one from IndusInd Bank; and the other from a Micro Finance Institution leading the Technology initiative. As of now, six Executives and Administrative Officers support the top management.

HR is its core asset and the driving force. Capital issues need resolution. Yet we moved along. Mere counselling and handholding revived 33 units during the last six months. Eighteen power loom units were assisted with margin funding for OTS itself and they are now on the path of revival. Recent valuation of the firm revealed a mark up by 100 per cent.

Microsoft and Syscon Solutions are its technology partners. FINTECH TIHCL went online on 25th June 2019, the first anniversary day. Technology is currently under testing process.

The structural innovation amply proves the need for progressive politician and proactive bureaucracy working together for a transparent, responsible and responsive institution to come up. The journey has just begun.

16

Renowned Industry Practices: Case Studies

Excellence is a journey and not a destination. Learning from the best practices would help upcoming enterprises choose and adapt them to their requirements. Therefore, every enterprise must find a fit with its own environment as what is best in a particular industry may not prove the best under different circumstances. Similarly, across the industry also best practices would change. Policies also impact differently on different enterprises and various types of entrepreneurs. It is important to see and analyse what suits them most and measure the extent to which such best practices should be transmitted to their own environment. Every such practice has its costs and returns and the entrepreneur should weigh his options very carefully so that adoption of best practices would add value in the entire production chain. Following case studies illustrate such practices in the supply chain, human resource, management and finance.

Case Study 1: RASI FLOWCHAINS LTD.

Outlook	Key Risk Factors
Rasi Flowchains Ltd was a small enterprise partnership venture incorporated in 1980 and was engaged in design, manufacture and distribution of high-tech industrial valves for domestic and international markets. Over the last 20 years, RFL had been providing valves for various end-uses and applications in refineries, petrochemicals, fertilizers, sugar, paper, steel, cement, chemical and pharmaceutical industries as well as in power plants around the world. The firm is certified by TUV Rheinland Group, a leading provider of technical services worldwide (advising, developing, promoting, examining and certifying) and other reputed buyers. RFL is committed to achieving customer satisfaction through meeting their requirements by adopting National & International Standards. Consistent maintenance of quality, timely delivery, fair pricing policy and wide range of options offered to buyers has contributed to growth and success. RFL has developed quality manual and procedure for its entire operations.	***Human Resource Quality*** The managing partner is the only person who has more than 25 years' experience in procurement of raw material, product designing and drawing. The firm is entirely dependent on the managing partner for designing and drawing. There was an absence of second line staff to take charge of the entire operations of the firm. ***Limits to growth:*** The firm drew its boundaries of growth at its current level of operations and would also like to make it more equity based than debt-based by clearing off its current liabilities as early as possible.

Staff retention, in-house training to staff, ensuring quality production, avoiding wastage and minimising rejections are major strengths. During the last three years the firm has achieved 10 per cent growth in terms of profits and expects to continue the same in the future. The financial figures for the year 2007 from the provisional (un-audited) balance sheet and Profit & Loss account was adjusted by DRS as the firm could provide only the sales, purchase and operating expenses for the financial year ending March 2007	

Best Practices

Staff Retention	All the staff members in RFL have been working there for more than five years; it is because of the freedom and accountability entrusted to each of the staff in the firm. The management pays attention in hiring the right people, trusting them and follows formal staff training and career development procedures, provides pleasant working condition and encourages team working and staff involvement.
Capacity Building	RFL provides in-house training to all the staff at each level of production to ensure quality production, avoid wastage and reduce rejections. It further ensures continuous improvement by practising QMS in technology, manufacturing, training and providing suitable resources.

Raw Material	RFL procures only quality and standard spares and raw material from local suppliers. The supply of raw material to each section is systematised at all levels of production. Regular house-keeping is done by each section staff after every shift.
Cost Reduction Strategy	When the cost of raw material gets increased, proportionately sale price is increased keeping the processing charges unchanged and also by effective utilisation of manpower and control over other overheads.
Strategy for Sustainability	RFL sells its products to reputed corporate bodies dealing in various sectors. It is committed to achieving customer satisfaction through meeting their requirements by adopting National & International Standards, timely delivery and reasonable price. Every valve manufactured is tested according to strict quality standards which ensure durable and trouble-free performance with low maintenance cost.

Triggers for adoption of Best Practices

Ravi, a Diploma holder in Mechanical Engineering, started his career by setting up an industry under the 20-Point Economic Programme initiated by erstwhile Prime Minister Indira Gandhi under the 'Self-Employment for Educated Unemployed Youths' (SEEUY) scheme.

The firm received subsidy loan from State Bank of India under the above scheme and purchased lathe machine and started the business of design and manufacture of valves. Ravi was the sole person to design/draw, purchase raw material and used to work on the machine to develop the valves. Labour problem, marketing and poor planning were the problems faced by him.

Over a period, he realised that customer relations and staff retention are the prime factors to enable him continue the business. Customers from various industries such as petrochemicals, fertilizers, sugar, paper, steel, cement, chemical and pharmaceutical have approached the enterprise to scale up their designs or improve their production processes.

Case Study 2: TRINITY ELECTRIC LINES PVT LTD.

Outlook

In 1920, Trilok Chand set up a trading business of electrical appliances in the name of Trilok Chand & Sons in Lahore, India, before Independence. Post-Independence, in 1959, the company's name was changed to Trinity and it established a manufacturing range of rewirable Switch Fuse Units (SFUs). In 1980, the company shifted its business to New Delhi, India,and started manufacturing of custom-built switchgears and by 1989 it had set up a 4,000 sq.m. plant in Sahibabad, Ghaziabad. Again, in 2005 and 2006, the company set up a satellite assembly unit of 4,050 sq.m. and 2,000 sq.m. (rented) at Manesar and in 2007, it set up a fabrication plant of 5,600 sq.m. adjacent to the Manesar plant.

Present

Trinity Electric Lines Private Limited (TEI) is (1) one of the leading manufacturers of custom-built low-tension switchboards and control gears; (2) is in trading of automatic transfer switches and compact sandwich busducts and (3) in contracting of erection and commissioning of electric substations (MV & HT). Trinity is professionally managed, customer driven, committed to total quality and constantly strives to exalt its customers by anticipating and exceeding their expectations through continuous improvement in the products and services that has paved the way to growth of the company.

Trinity proudly presents itself as the All India distributors of Power Plug Busduct (World renowned Malaysian manufacturer of Busway Trunking System) with sophisticated thermodynamic design applications and quality manufacturing methods to deliver good performance products. In the trading sector, the company products are the Emerson Networks, ASCO automatic transfer switches and are executed to various reputed customers such as Tata Consultancy,

Tata Tele Services, Bharti Tele Services, DFL, American Express, Xansa India Ltd., Delhi and Hyderabad Airports, Bhushan Steel & Strips, DLF, Wipro, Adobe, IBM, NTPC and ITC among others.

Trinity is an ISO 9001:2000 BVQI and also ISO 14001:2004 BVQI certified company and they are now in the process of getting Integrated Management Systems Certificate from BVQI.

Trinity follows a good HR policy, provides interest-free loans to staff, has a separate training & development facility, good library, online 360° appraisal system. Trinity also conducts health camps, tree plantations, festival celebrations, team building excursions and recreations. Its strength lies in coping with competition from its elder brother L&T Switchgears.

The growth of the company for the last three years: Annual sales and fixed assets increased by more than 100 per cent. Net profit after tax and interest for the year 2007 increased by more than 10 times compared to the year 2006. Technology and market risks are foreseeable.

Best Practices

TQM	The company dedicates itself to total quality and constantly strives to exalt the customers by anticipating and exceeding their expectations. Continuous improvement, teamwork, commitment, integrity and excellence are the company's guiding values. Onsite & offsite customer training are regularly conducted. QMS was being implemented very well throughout the company. The company was a WASO 9001:2000 BVQI and also WASO 14001:2004 BVQI certified company and they got Integrated Management Systems Certificate from BVQI in 2007. The company had stringent QAP for consistency in Quality. Quality records to support compliance of QAP.

Machinery	The company had a well-equipped factory with all modern equipment comprising both Indian and foreign machines. CNC Turret Punch and NC Press Break are from AMADA, Japan; NC Shearing Press from BAKEL, Turkey; Busbar 3-in-1 press from SML, UK; Crimping Machine from CEMBRE, Italy; Paint Process GEMA, Switzerland and R.O. Plant from India. The company had also well-equipped research, design and development centre with latest CAD/CAM techniques and specially customised Elecdes software, resulting in immaculate engineering. Machines for manufacturing of dies, jigs, fixtures and SPM tools are developed in-house which leads to cost-effective solutions and total quality products.
Staff Retention through Good HR Practices – Transparency was the Hallmark in employee relations	There was good understanding and trust between the employer and the employees. The management provided good environment, working conditions, safety nets and pathway for career to the employees. The staff have been provided with suggestion scheme (suggestion box was placed), quality circles, weekly focus and daily morning meetings, training and development – competency mapping, career progression, knowledge management – e-library, global information on server and website, online 360°appraisal, employee welfare, in-house canteen facilities, interest-free loans, health camps, tree plantation programmes, in-house yoga and Vedanta classes, recreation clubs, team building activities and festival celebrations with family members. Trinity Quarterly Journals: Highlights of company's growth, R&D, new products, recreation programmes, staff best-liked performance awards, wedding, parenthood, years of service, birthdays, anniversaries, new joining and other information are provided on quarterly basis.

Cost Reduction Strategy through technology upgradation	Trinity has in-house facilities for research, design and development using CAD/CAM techniques and specially customised Elecdes software which results in immaculate engineering performance. Dies, jigs, fixtures & SPM tools are developed in-house which lead to cost-effective solutions, and quality product.
Strategy for Sustainability	The company strives to maintain and produce superior quality products, product improvement, dedicated customer care division with 24-hr helpline, enhance the capability of employees, staff appraisals and maximum utilisation of installed capacity. Committed to achieving customer satisfaction through meeting their requirements by adopting National & International Standards, timely delivery at an affordable price.

Case Study 3: DesignMake Solutions

Outlook

DesignMake was formed in 2001 by Desai and other two partners—experts in the fields of Mechanical Engineering, IT and Marketing, respectively. In 2004, one of the partners resigned and subsequently the name of the firm was changed from x to DesignMake CAD/CAM Solutions. The firm has both Indian and imported CNC machines and uses high-end software application for design and manufacture of tools, dies and moulds in a shorter period (one die/mould in three days rather than three months) with customer focus and higher specification and quality. The firm has an agency agreement of buying and selling of machines, its maintenance both in domestic and international markets and also supplies high-end imported software for CAD/CAM solutions with in-house training to its customers.

The firm has reputed customers such as The Supreme Industries, Godrej Boyce Mfg. Co., Philips (I) Ltd., Mutual Industries Ltd.

and SWECO (India) Pvt. Ltd. (a division of MI Drilling USA) and international customers from the US and France. The firm has grown very fast during the last three years (2004-07) as sales have gone up from Rs 34.7 lakh in 2005 to Rs 87.1 lakh in 2007, the fixed assets have increased from Rs 8.8 lakh to Rs 28.4 lakh and the net worth has increased from Rs 8.9 lakh to Rs 30.6 lakh as on March 2007. The major strength of the firm is design and making of higher specification tools, dyes and moulds with customer focus and staff retention through upgradation of new technology, performance-based incentives and providing training both locally as well as abroad. The financial figures for 2007 are from the audited balance sheet.

Best Practices

High Quality, Higher Specification Designs and Customer-focused solutions	The motive of DesignMake is to provide consolidated design and development services to the engineering industry with an emphasis on optimal designs of tools, dyes and moulds with cost-effective options and customer-focused solutions. The major strength of this firm is to provide quality services through integration of various technologies in designing and development of tools, dyes, moulds and offers complete CAD/CAM solutions for 2D-3D conversions, 3D modelling, Reverse Engineering, Deep drawing Articles, machining of large jobs on CNC machines and other job works. The firm is also engaged in selling of CNC machines, supply of software related to CAD/CAM solutions and provides in-house training on CAD/CAM to its customers. DesignMake attracts customers by quality presentation and demonstration of its product with best available machines.

Machinery	DesignMake had a well-equipped factory with both Indian and foreign CNC machines for design and development, higher specification dies and moulds and they also have a heavy-duty lathe machine for drilling. Air-conditioned CAD/CAM training centre for its customers with high-end software applications. DesignMake had entered into an agency agreement for selling machines manufactured by Lokesh Machines, Hyderabad; Hurco Machines Inc, USA; Lifton Magnets, Singapore and a JV with Evoque of Italy for its product development, presentation and designing.
Staff retention and capacity building	There is good understanding and trust between the employer and the employees. The team has been built over a period of five years and given the opportunity to grow and explore themselves in their respective fields and were provided training both locally and abroad. Training on new technology and innovations is upgraded periodically. Staff in the firm not only adhere to their routine work but also got the opportunity to learn and explore themselves by visiting the customers/vendors for marketing, maintenance, demo, presentation and leverage to price-fixing. Incentives are paid periodically based on sales, performance and subsequent appraisals are done every three to six months.
Cost Reduction Strategy through technology upgradation	DesignMake had imported CNC machine and use high-end CAD/CAM application (software) for designing the tools, dye and mould which had reduced the manpower cost and time reduction from three months to only three days for designing a single product.

Strategy for Sustainability	DesignMake wants to continue and retain customers by providing quality service and develop superior quality of products with cost reduction methodology, maximum utilisation of installed capacity, enhance the staff capability, increase sales of software and provide hand-holding services related to CAD/CAM solutions. Committed to achieve customer satisfaction through meeting their requirements by adopting National & International Standards, timely delivery at an affordable price.

Case Study 4: Dhanalaxmi Expo

Outlook	**Key Risk Factors**
Dhanalaxmi Expo is a partnership firm formed in 1990 by Mr S. Rama and Mr N. Sreedhar. Both the partners, operating as a buying agency, were actively involved in the business of providing service to the potential buyers and fashion houses globally to supply them according to their design and order high quality men, women and children's fashion wear. In 1997, another partner Mr Tamizharasan, an expert in fashion designing and printing, joined the firm and they setup a manufacturing unit and started exporting knitwear in 1998. Dhanalaxmi Expo emphasises on dedication, quality, high professionalism and top notch designing to provide high quality and remarkable service. Dhanalaxmi Expo ensures that every level of production is controlled with thorough quality checks to make sure that the fabric of every garment produced is in accordance with international standards. The firm had acquired high quality imported dyeing, cutting and	Forex Risk and Manpower Risk

soft squeezing machines and started three more units by 2006. The firm is 100 per cent export-oriented, has strong hold in Europe, the US and Canada and aspire to venture and penetrate all markets of the world. The firm purchases yarn from the local market and sends samples to the customers. After approving the customers provide the shades, design and various sizes to make readymade garments. The firm had recruited qualified pattern masters, Quality Control managers and purchasers. The firm had grown very fast during the four years (2004, 05, 06 & 07) as the sales have gone up from Rs 1,297.6 lakh in 2004 to Rs 2,620.6 lakh in 2007, fixed assets increased from Rs 228.2 lakh to Rs 1,356.2 lakh and the net worth increased from Rs 342.4 lakh to Rs 819.3 lakh as on March 2007. All the three partners have equal share of the profit in the firm. The financial figures for 2007 are from the provisional (un-audited) balance sheet provided by the firm.	

Best Practices

High Quality & use of technology in processing the textiles.	Dhanalaxmi Expo ensures that every level of production goes through thorough quality checks to make sure that the fabric of every garment produced is in accordance with international standards. The firm had acquired various capacities of dyeing machines to keep the fabric in its original nature (Knits are known for their elasticity) and also cater to the need of smallest quantity to bulk production without hampering the shade and quality. Quality had been given prime preference and world class products include polyester and its blends with Lycra, cotton and Lycra, Viscose and Lycra blends being processed very easily and delivered on time.

Machinery	Dhanalaxmi Expo has a well-equipped factory with imported machineries from Greece, Italy, Sweden and Germany. They have a Sclavos Soft Flow dyeing machine to handle the knitted fabrics very gently and keep its original nature. It has self-cleaning and rinsing facility; consumes less water for processing and produces very less quantity of effluent when compared to conventional machineries. Calator Balloon Squeezer: This machine is from Sweden which had a specialised Roborto roller for soft squeezing of the delicate knitted fabrics. The main feature of this roborto roller is that no padding mark is permanent after squeezing. The padding lines disappear during subsequent drying and compacting processes. Santex Relax Drier: This machine is from Italy and used for drying the fabric to its necessary limit and has a special feature in which tumbling device is provided for reducing the shrinkage of the fabric in drying stage itself. Slit opening: Bianco, an Italian made machine, cuts the fabric very precisely where it has to be opened for further lay cutting. The speed of the machine is approximately 100 mtr./min. Babcock Stenter: It is a German make machine in which the width of the machine is well controlled. Certain fabrics are cut after stentering without compacting since the shrinkage is controlled in stentering stage itself. Also, this machine is particularly very much helpful in special finishing like anti-microbial, soil release finish, Wicking finish for polyester, flame retardant finish etc., It is a very versatile machine to handle woven and knits.

Staff Retention and Capacity Building	The permanent staff of Dhanalaxmi Expo has good understanding and trust between the employer and the employees. The team is built over a period of six years and has been given the opportunity to grow and explore themselves in their respective field and were provided trainings in procurement of yarns, designing on CAD, dyeing and quality control. Training on new technology and innovations is upgraded periodically. Incentives are paid periodically based on performance.
Cost Reduction Strategy through technology upgradation	As already mentioned, Dhanalaxmi Expo has imported automated cutting machines which are operated through high-end CAD/CAM application and can cut up to 50,000 pieces at a time. Designing is also done on this CAD/CAM application. This not only reduces the cost of manpower in cutting but also avoids rejections and has quality cuttings.
Strategy for Sustainability	Dhanalaxmi Expo wants to continue and retain its customers by manufacturing high quality readymade garments, high professionalism, latest design, and timely delivery as per customer satisfaction. Enhancement of the factory by adding latest technology in dyeing, cutting and quality check before cutting the fabrics with cost reduction methodology, maximum utilisation of installed capacity, and capability building of staff for new technologies. Ensuring that every level of production is controlled with thorough quality checks to make sure that the fabric of every garment produced is in accordance with international standards.

Case Study 5: DUTTU SOLUTIONS

Outlook B.S. Sathe, the Scientific Officer from Tata Institute of Fundamental Research (TIFR), established Duttu Solutions in 1960. While working in TIFR, he started making scientific equipment for school laboratories which he used to supply to the schools locally. As the operations increased, he quit his job in 1967, and setup a small household enterprise for manufacturing primary kits (demonstration kit for school laboratories) and also started manufacturing transistor-based power supply units. **Growth Process** During 1976, Thamank, a Diploma holder in Mechanical Engineering and Sathe's nephew, joined the enterprise and increased sales through marketing the products in all the schools in and around Bombay. The industry expanded by purchasing land, procurement of lathe machine, drilling machine and welding machine for large-scale manufacturing of products. The business was diversified from schools to industries. Meanwhile, P.S. Agwan, BE Mechanical from Nagpur, an employee of L&T and Sathe's tenant, married his daughter and joined the business in 1981. Having experience in drawing, designing and manufacturing of tools and the ability to provide solutions to customer-oriented problems, Agwan took the initiative of manufacturing Heavy Duty Tubular Gauges. The industry prepared a very good catalogue with support from technical persons and advertised in *The Times of India*; got mileage from more than 350 clients for the products. The industry started manufacturing other products such	**Key Risk Factors** Aversion to vertical growth

as Displacer transmitters, Liquid Level Gauges, Magnetic Indicators, Level Switches Manometers and Sight Glasses. Agwan travelled almost 1 lakh km in two years on a scooter to market the products and also providing handholding services to the customers.

Joint Venture

From 1992 to 2000, the industry had a JV with a Swiss company to supply Electric Bend components for Displacer Transmitters and this product was sold in the company's brand name. During 1989 to 2001, three more technical persons from the same family joined the business and after acquiring thorough knowledge of the technicality of the products, and expiry of JV with the Swiss company, each individual had setup their own unit and were enjoying the business by outsourcing the job works within the four units.

Uniqueness

The USP of Duttu Solutions is its BPO model in the SME sector for outsourcing the job works of the products, assemble and deliver to the customers from within the group. If any cheaper components of the products are available in the market, the industry is not interested to produce in its workshop. All the four sister-concern industries minimise the outflow of resources and also the growth of the industry. The group does not want to grow vertically but is growing horizontally and is focused on per employee output of minimum of Rs 8 to 10 lakh per year.

Best Practices

Goodwill, Customer Satisfaction & Strict adherence to Regulatory Compliance,	The goodwill of the industry in manufacturing scientific equipment for school laboratories and providing solutions to teachers by way of providing required equipment for teaching methodology at school level was one of the core strengths of the industry during the initial stage i.e. during 1960s. Duttu Solutions, pioneer in the field of Magnetic Indicators with application-oriented R&D as its strength, went on to develop several state-of-the-art instruments for the first time in India – like Magnetic Indicator for Liquid Chlorine-Magnamount, intrinsically safe transmitter for LPG - Insertrans, Bicoloured magnetic indication-Rotocyl, Displacer type Indicating Transmitter-Immertrans or Helitrans - LVDT—all with 100 per cent indigenous know-how. The major strength of this enterprise is providing quality services through integration of various technologies in designing and development of tools. It offers complete solution to the customers with regard to the machines and other job-works. Duttu believes and attracts customers by quality presentation and demonstration of its product with best available machines. The group strictly adheres to the 100 percent Regulatory Compliance about staff structure, taxes, and other legal procedures of the Industrial Legislation.
Machinery	S. J. Duttu had a well-equipped factory with heavy lathe machines, drilling and welding machines. In addition, it had special purpose machines and special quality assurance equipment, which

	ensures consistent quality and timely delivery. The work is manned by highly qualified managerial staff and skilled workmen. The office is equipped with computers in local area network, with access to each staff member.
Cost Reduction Strategy	The price range of S. J. Duttu is always competitive in the market. However, ensuring quality products and services remain its primary concern. S. J. Duttu provides hand-holding services to the customers and charges minimum to attract them for further services. It believes in volumes and quality.
Strategy for Sustainability	S. J. Duttu wants to continue outsourcing job works for cheaply available components in the market, retaining the customers by providing quality service and developing superior quality of products with cost reduction strategies, maximum utilisation of installed capacity, enhancing staff capability, increasing sales, and providing hand-holding services. It is committed to achieving customer satisfaction through meeting their requirements by adopting National & International Standards and timely delivery at an affordable price. Initially, the unit was purchasing the required components for magnetic indicators and other measuring instruments from outsiders. It realised that it was losing out on margins. Strategically, they moved for backward integration by setting up units to manufacture the components required within the group. Having set up two such units, it felt the need for having an accounting firm which then Mrs P.S. Agwan started.

Case Study 6: WATER Industries Limited

Products and Services	• Hook and Loop tape fasteners · Knitted Elastics · Woven Elastic · Braided Products · Webbing · Satin ribbons and checks ribbons

Best Practices

Marketing	The company's major strength lies in marketing and brand positioning. The management of WATER believes that this is a unique opportunity for it to participate in the establishment of a new and large underserved channel of distribution for their products. The company had the ability to deliver the products according to customer requirements in quality, different shades and in huge quantity.
Customer Satisfaction	The company continuously strives towards excellence, nurturing a futuristic outlook. Innovation and stringent quality control measures combined with dynamic marketing approach and professional customer service helped the group to establish a strong customer base. Complete customer satisfaction had always been the group's motto. The company considers quality consciousness as the key requirement for the products and services.
Machinery	The company had latest infrastructure and is equipped with 66 imported needle loom machines, high voltage generator, and centrally air-conditioned computer room with high-end CAD/CAM applications. Shamots Needle Looms for narrow fabric machines in a completely knocked-down condition are also imported and

	assembled at the Daman plant, which gave the company its competitive edge in the local market. Rigorous quality control is maintained, and products conform to international standards.
Staff Retention	Staff retention through good HR practices: The company had developed an operational manual (induction manual) which is transparent and circulated to all the employees that consists of detailed objectives of the company's vision and mission, company policies and procedures, staff benefits and growth perspective. Employee satisfaction: Creating an environment where staff members enjoy their work and realise their full potential; find opportunities to grow; focus their attention on satisfying customer-needs, thus creating commitment to customers and, therefore, to the organisation. The company follows an open culture, informal and non-bureaucratic approach which encourages continuous learning and enhancing the image of the company as a world class company. Encourages team work, along with individual excellence, develops a sense of belonging amongst employees by caring attitude. Believes in following well-documented standard procedures and systems in the day-to-day working. Builds enough flexibility to encourage and accommodate innovative thoughts. Institutes fair and equitable system to reward employees according to their contribution. Considers employees as valued assets. Promotes commitment and creativity for better performance. Encourages employees to take a part of superior's responsibility, while at the same time develops subordinates such that all the three would be ready to take up still higher responsibility as and when required (a sort of push-and-pull theory).

Cost Reduction Strategy	The company takes feedback of staff on internal policies, target orientation, etc., and upgrades the machines with latest technology, scales up the production through adding one more belt (from 4 to 5 strips) for maximum utilisation of installed capacity and by minimising wastage.
Strategy for Sustainability	WATER industries want to continue and retain its customers by providing variety of superior quality products according to customer specifications with cost reduction methodology, maximum utilisation of installed capacity, enhancing the staff capability and increasing sales.

Case Study 7: R.R. PLASTOS, Hyderabad

Outlook	Key Risk Factors
Origin R.R. Plastos was set up by Mr Seshagiri Rao in 1988. Due to lack of technology, poor management, bad reputation with the creditors, materials supplied to the vendors were rejected. Bad quality, lack of right source for raw-material and involvement in politics rendered the industry sick by 1995. The ratio of assets vs. liability was 1:3. **Growth Process:** Revival, Reconstruction and Building Trust The company that was on the brink of collapse could be rejuvenated through a series of measures: change in management and relationships; investments in assets of quality; ploughing back profits into the firm by acquisition of landed property that could also serve as additional collateral for financing institutions, creating confidence in the product through assurance of quality and delivery, incentivising product pickup	The Company had to invest in IPRs

through lavish sample deliveries and ensuring prompt client response. Getting a worthwhile rating was the beginning of getting into new markets and establishing a niche for itself. In 1996-97, realising the product value and demand in the market, Mr G.Venkateshwarlu, the then Managing Director, took over the company by investing Rs 20 lakh along with his sister. The amount was used for re-alignment and modification of machines, payment of staff salaries and payment to creditors with an understanding that they will start supplying the raw materials. The company's name was changed from S.S. Rubbers & Plastic Products to R.R. Plastos in 1998. (During this period 1996-1998, the turnover was Rs 17 lakh).

1998 to 2001: Mr G. Venkateshwarlu took over the entire operations (Mr Seshagiri Rao left the company) and in the process it took nearly two-and-a-half years to recover and improve the business; purchased land (on subsidy); recruited new technical staff; capacity building to previous staff, frequent visits to the previous vendors to market and distributed free samples of quality product to re-build trust and receive orders. The turnover increased to Rs 1 crore.

2002 to 2006: Started purchasing raw material from import dealers to improve the quality of product; purchased additional land in the industrial area; old machines were modified and new machines with latest technology were purchased; visited new clients to market the products; designed and developed moulds and seals according to customer specification and imported calibrated equipment for quality testing. Sales have been doubled from the previous years; this is due to the rebuilding of trust from the old clients and receiving repeat orders from old clients and new orders from new ones.

Best Practices

Customer Specification & Satisfaction	R.R.Plastos was committed to producing quality products while confirming to relevant specifications, standards and have built a high level of confidence and satisfaction in customers. The objectives are achieved through continued improvement, upgradation of technology and resources based on quality management system.
Product Design	R.R.Plastos have developed a successful design of oil seals both of split, solid in single and dual lip type genres with different polymers like Flouro Elastomer silicon Polychloroprene, Acrylonitrile etc. Factors like temperature, pressure, relative motion and operating conditions which influence the performance and life of the seal are considered while selecting the material and design of the seal. Generally, the materials used for oil seals are Flouro Elastomer and Silicone.
Diverse range of Quality products	R.R. Plastos supply a diverse range of products servicing a variety of markets such as thermal power plants, Indian defence industry, cement industry, other power generation plants and commercial segments. The company had specialised in designing the product and can manufacture the product as per customer requirement in any size and specifications. The company had established ISO 9001 – 2000 Quality Management System.

Machinery	R.R. Plastos was equipped with local and imported machines. They have imported two PLC controlled compression moulding machines from Germany and one from Belgaum (India), lathe machines for tool manufacturing and quality testing machines such as Endurance Testing Machine for supplying oil seals only after conducting thorough test (type test & routine test) as per standards, and also equipped with 5,000 kg Micro Universal Testing Bench, Oscillating Disc Rheometer, Electronic Densimeter, Abrasion Strength testing Machine and other testing equipment.
Strategy for Cost Reduction	Reducing wastage and rejection, change of technology to scale up and speed up the production by installing latest machines, recruitment of technical staff, providing capacity building to staff to latest technology, improvement in inventory of holding raw material and finished stocks are some of the cost reduction strategies adopted by the company.
Staff Retention and Capacity Building	R.R.Plastos did not let the old staff (who worked when the company was sick) to leave the company, but provided training to upgrade their skills to match the latest technology and provided them free environment to continue in the company. The company maintains a good HR practice by providing all the statutory requirements of the employees such as ESI, PF, timely payment of salary, leave, annual appraisals etc. There are some 8 to 10 staff who are still continuing in the company for more than a decade.

Case Study 8: Bhuwan Engineering Private Limited Best Practices

Customer Satisfaction, Quality and Perfection and User-friendly Machines	Bhuwan Engineering Private Limited strives to provide innovative solutions and bring in latest technology, advanced products and services to the customers. The industry believes that this was possible due to their single-minded mission of providing total customer satisfaction by delivering products and services that consistently exceed the customer expectations. The goal of Bhuwan Engineering was **'Quality in Quantity and Perfection in Performance'**, the customer should get more worth than the value paid, and they do provide it. The industry ensures that machines supplied to the customers are user-friendly and there was no need for maintenance, and if any minor problems arose, the customer can resolve them on their own (problem-free machines). The industry obtained the certification of ISO 9002 to improve the manufacturing process implementing the quality management system very strictly. The industry quotes 'Our endeavour was to perform and change to our customers' requirement. A change which we anticipate, manage and adopt to help our customers perform more efficiently'.
Machinery	Bhuwan Engineering was equipped with imported machines from Germany, Korea and Taiwan for the purpose of GIC boring and for manufacturing components. Hindustan Machine Tools (HMT-manufactured machines are purchased in scrap, then they are re-conditioned and re-aligned according to the industry requirement and are used for drilling, milling and turning. They

	have also acquired a heavy-duty lathe machine. Overall, the industry had acquired about 20 machines and 15 machines out of them were purchased during the last three years.
Staff Retention and Capacity building	Bhuwan Engineering maintained a good HR practice in industry. Staff retention by providing free environment, capacity building on innovative and new products, annual appraisals, celebration of festivals; considering the problems of staff in and out of industry. Suggestions from employees are considered and justified, staff incentives for innovative work, bonus, ESI and other statutory benefits are in place. All the senior staff in the industry are there since its inception and other technical staff, i.e. fitters, turners, millers etc. are working with the firm for more than five years.
Technology	The industry had developed wrapping machine which is designed to wrap cigarettes with BOPP film to protect the aroma of cigarette inside and it is fitted with latest technology to run totally Automatic Machine Auto in-feed System, Pneumatic Exit and with many more safety features to match international standards.

Case Study 9: ATC Engineering Company

Best Practices

High Quality, Higher Specification and Customer-Oriented	The main strength of ATC Engineering was customer retention at the height of competition. ATC Engineering is providing services to the entire BHEL throughout India and other reputed corporate bodies through

	quality Bending of Pipes and Plates as per customer satisfaction. The company can take up high fabrication job-works such as X-ray quality welding by Argon and ARC process with stringent control measures. QMS is being implemented very well throughout the Company. The Company is I.B.R. Approved ISO 9001-2000 Registered and also got approved by the Chief Inspector of Boilers, Tamil Nadu for manufacture of Pressure Parts and Pipe Bends. ATC believes and attract customers by quality practice and timely delivery of product with best available machines.
Machinery	ATC Engineering had a well-equipped workshop with the following machines: Plate bending machine capacity 25mm thick x 2500 mm width, pipe bending machine electro-pneumatic capacity up to 76mm diameter, hydro bend pipe bending machine up to 6-inch diameter, hot bending arrangement capacity up to 12-inch diameter pipe, furnace, welding generators, rectifiers and transformers and argon welding set, radial drilling machine capacity 40mm, band saw cutting machine, lifting arrangement up to 10-tonne capacity and 62.5 KVA power generator.
Cost Reduction Strategy	ATC Engineering had a strategy of performing job-works through contract employees (outsourced). There was no risk of absenteeism, strike and wage increments. This resulted in maximum utilisation of machinery and labour. Raw material is supplied by the customer for job-works, Pipe or Plate Bending

	specifications/dimension (Sample) is given to the shift-in-charge to monitor other employees in the shift. Likewise fabrication specification was also provided according to customer requirement. The company is backed by dedicated skilled workforce including I.B.R. qualified welders. Capacity building is provided to permanent staff when necessary at the time of new job-works undertaken.
Strategy for Sustainability	ATC Engineering wanted to continue and retain customers by providing quality service, timely delivery of goods and at an affordable price. Manufacturing superior quality of products with cost reduction methodology, reducing rejections and wastage, maximum utilisation of installed capacity, capacity building to staff, and providing hand-holding services related to customer-driven specifications. Committed to achieve customer satisfaction through meeting their requirements and also providing new technologies/designing from external agencies.

17

Organisation Failures: Case Studies

Failure is not bad if one learns lessons from it and makes appropriate corrections at the right time. However, it is difficult initially to admit failure; and much more difficult, and sometimes costly, to change the ways of doing things the entrepreneur has been accustomed to for a long time until he noticed serious erosion in the balance sheet of his enterprise. The entrepreneur does not care for a headache until it keeps surfacing frequently. Thereafter he feels stressful every day while running the enterprise. But rarely does he know the reason for such headache, nor does he feel the need to approach for resolution at the hands of an expert. It could be also that he is afraid of either due to presumptive loss of prestige or the cost involved.

Stress can come from anywhere for the enterprise and at any point of time. But recognising the source of such stress would be generally beyond the entrepreneur because of the markets and environment or ignoring the happenings within the industry. People are generally viewed as a great resource in an industry compared to the machines. Most small entrepreneurs tend to ignore the cultural moorings of people working with them. They also tend to ignore some valuable suggestions coming from the people handling the machines. The shop floor person knows much more than the owner. But this is rarely recognised. The entrepreneur also tends to overestimate his capacities compared to the industry capacities. Instead of starting the unit looking at the market, he invariably looks at his own competence to produce and feels that what he produces should be picked up by the market. The latter just does not happen in open markets. The following case studies illustrate many of such failures only with a view to finding right solutions and not to discourage the entrepreneurs in this vital sector of the economy.

Case Study 1: PETROL SPILLS

Sri Vignana Petro Products Pvt Ltd

The unit's proprietor Mr Agarwal was into manufacturing and distribution of oils and other petroleum products. He was also distributor of major engine oil brands like Servo, Laal Ghoda etc. He entered business after completing his higher secondary. His forefathers had started this business and it being a family business, he did not undergo any professional training. As a result of this, there is lack of professionalism in the management. He employed around 50 workers and the business is carried on entirely based on the family expertise in the domain and with indigenous technology. The business was going well until the MNCs started giving tough competition. Lack of brand image for the products of Vignana Petro coupled with the company's inability to advertise their products had resulted in loss of markets. The company, therefore, had to lower its prices because of which the profit margins got lowered drastically and the company became sick.

The unit had gone into problems because of intense competition from MNCs in the post-liberalisation period and did not have resources to fight the competition by investing in advertising and brand-building. The unit approached the APSSIRS with the promise to repay debts: (i) by using on-hand rate contract with APSRTC for re-procuring used lubricating engine oils from various depots (ii) by concentrating on wholesale markets and (iii) by diverting attention to bulk buyers/ institutional customers. After discussions with SBI, the Commissioner of Industries gave the Rehabilitation package on 28-10-2002, whereat the unit agreed to give post-dated cheques for repayment of interest and agreed to pay arrears within five years. The Banker was required to give six months' time to the unit and to watch the performance. Despite having agreed to do so, the Banker committed a breach of understanding by filing a case against the unit in the DRT.

The unit had to down its shutters. Banks did not even acknowledge the letters received even to the top brass, leave alone informing action taken on the complaint. If it is a complaint on e-mail, a standard reply of acknowledgement—system driven—appears that the matter would be attended in 24/8 hours.

Case Study 2: INCIPIENT SICKNESS LEAKS IN THE PIPE PLUGGED

Sai Industries Pvt. Ltd.

Satyasundar purchased a unit manufacturing stoneware pipes and refractors in 1988 and re-named it as **Sai Industries Pvt. Ltd.** He contracted a term loan of Rs 18 lakh on the day of taking over which escalated to Rs 58 lakh by 1996. His term loan liability was closed under OTS with APSFC. Later, he started Banking with Andhra Bank and took a Term Loan of Rs 16 lakh for modernisation, Rs 15 lakh for trading and Rs 9.5 lakh as working capital.

The unit ran into problems because of certain expected orders not materialising in respect of drainage and sewerage works. The firm was supplying material to Visakhapatnam Municipal Corporation and Vizianagaram and Srikakulam Municipalities for underground drainage and other related works. The project of Visakhapatnam Municipal Corporation, estimated at Rs 20 crore with purchase of stoneware pipes worth Rs 5 crore, was postponed.

This postponement led to the unit turning sick and the account became NPA by 28-03-2002. The unit quickly diversified its activity to PVC pipes and fittings trade since July 2002 and, by January 2003, it could generate income to regularise its Term Loan account. The firm's request for rescheduling the Term Loan was considered favourably by the Banker because of the promise generated out of renewed contracts from the Visakhapatnam Municipal Corporation. The Bank also waived penal interest and re-credited the excess penal charges to the account.

This is a case where the Bank took interest in a proactive manner and upgraded the Sub-standard Asset to Standard Asset.

Case Study 3: SMAAT Smitten

Smaat India Private Limited was a social enterprise in the Micro and Small Enterprise sector set up with the objective of providing safe drinking water solutions to rural communities across the country. It manufactures, installs and maintains eco-friendly, user-friendly, cost-effective water treatment plants using non-chemical technologies, generating local employment in large numbers.

In response to a tender call from the Chief Engineer, Department of Panchayat Raj (PRED), Bangalore dated 30-05-2011 from registered, reputed firms/NGOs/consortia to procure, install, commission, operate and maintain for a period of 10 years by collecting user charges for fluoride/arsenic/TDS removal water treatment plants with various investment options, Smaat India as a successful L-1 bidder under BOOT option had been allotted the work for only 400 plants out of total 3,000 plants for providing 10 LPCD per person per day to the community size of 500 to 25,000 persons.

After successful installation of five plants on pilot basis in Gadag district, an agreement was entered into with Executive Engineer, PRED in respect of each village for setting up of Community Water Centres in accordance with the tender specifications.

The PRED failed to honour its following principal obligations provided under clause 1.1 of the Main Clauses of Agreement at its own cost that resulted in loss of user charges that formed the economic basis of investment:

1. Appropriate Raw Water Source, which shall meet the Raw Water Specifications, in sufficient quantities to meet the demand for Purified Water from the Community Water Systems.
2. A Site which shall meet the Site Specifications should be suitable to Smaat India for the installation of the Community Water Systems.
3. An electricity connection of adequate load, whose consumption charges will be borne by Smaat India.

On the brink of collapse of the enterprise financially, Smart had approached the MSME Facilitation Council, Government of Telangana for justice. This was a typical case of government playing the role of a buyer, government-owned bank financing the enterprise and government playing the role of arbitrator over non-payment of dues to the company. The Karnataka Government preferred to approach the High Court of Karnataka over a settled issue in the MSME Development Act regarding the jurisdiction of the MSE Facilitation Council in passing the orders. The Court gave an interim stay. All the cases are being contested by the unit.

The unit in the meantime got the tag of NPA with blockage of operations in the account in Andhra Bank. Andhra Bank did a TEV study at a cost of Rs 6 lakh and found the unit fit for rehabilitation.

One of the conditions of rehabilitation is that the unit brings 25 per cent of the nearly Rs 60 crore as margin money for rehabilitation. If the unit had this much cash, it would have rolled over in multiples even without the bank support. It was the case of delayed decision and that too an inappropriate one. The entrepreneur, with his unflinching loyalty to the financing bank, was firm on repaying the debt in toto by realising the judgement debtors sooner than later and calling quits to bank debt!!

During the 10-year standing of his account with Andhra Bank, the bank never troubled him until the Karnataka Government defaulted on its PPP agreements and deprived him of revenue. On the other hand, the Bank took pride in carrying the unit's caricature in its news bulletins and supported the 'safe drinking water mission' of the company beyond banking. Now the same bank had served a notice of default under SARFAESI Act. The Damocles' sword is on his neck. Several private investors were in line for evaluation as the sector—'Water'–had a live potential as long as universe exists.

The entrepreneur, highly innovative with 153 international and national awards featuring on **Fords Front Page** twice, entertained hopes of turning around. Karunakar Reddy, the innovative entrepreneur, was on a mission mode in opening new verticals like **99k walk for water**, rejuvenation of dried up bore wells with a three-year warranty and Water ATM installations. CSR funding was also explored.

The Bank in the instant case tried its best to help the unit. But it cannot be expected to hold the umbrella for long. Thanks to the IBC, the case was transferred to the NCLT after the unit filed for bankruptcy.

Case Study 4: THE SCALES TILT

Tulsi Hindustan Ltd.

Prabhakar, a graduate in Mechanical Engineering was a trained tool room engineer. Prior to starting the unit, he worked with Hyderabad Allwyn, Hindustan Motors and Republic Forge. He worked for some years in France before starting the unit. He, being a technocrat, prepared the project report for the unit with his own expertise. The unit started its commercial production in 1968 and it was the first unit to start production of weighing machines in India. With an investment of Rs 11 crore, this does not qualify for being defined as SSI. The unit's accumulated cash losses as on 31-03-2003 were Rs 10 crore. There was inordinate delay in accounts receivables from Bhilai Steel Company and the Prompt Payments Act did not come to his rescue, he bemoans. He is fully knowledgeable and had enough business acumen.

As a result, the unit plunged into sickness during late 1980s. This was a medium sized industry. Further mistrust of commercial banks regarding sick units and bureaucracy interfering in the day-to-day activities of the business are further leading to inefficient working of the SSI, he avers.

Case Study 5: MATTRESSES SHRINK

Comfort Industries Ltd.

M/s Comfort Industries Limited, formerly known as Bhargava Industries Ltd. was established in 1994, to manufacture, under the brand name 'KOZYLON'. The Brand was well accepted in Andhra Pradesh, Tamil Nadu, Kerala, Odisha, Madhya Pradesh and parts of Maharashtra. In the past eight years, it had become one of the market leaders in the captioned industry. In 1998, to cater to the additional demand, Narayana, the Chief Promoter of Comfort Industries Ltd., started another company at Gudiwada, M/s Comfort Coir Products Limited, to manufacture the same product. To cater to the markets in Maharashtra, Madhya Pradesh, Karnataka, Goa, Gujarat and other northern states besides some parts of Andhra Pradesh, the group established another unit at Hyderabad.

The company had an excellent infrastructure to manufacture good quality mattresses with a total asset base of around Rs 25 crore which includes 16 acres of land and 3 lakh sq.ft. of construction in which both the units are housed besides the plant & machinery. The company owns two imported PU foam plants and imported quilting and tape edging machines.

The company at 80 per cent of its installed capacity can manufacture 4.32 lakh mattresses per annum with a capability to achieve a turnover of around Rs 88 crore with a net profit of around Rs 6.25 crore. The product attracts a Sales Tax of 12 per cent in Andhra Pradesh and 4-13 per cent in other states. The company had a good dealer network and commands good reputation in the market for its products. However, its over-ambition to expand capacities without concern to the liquidity for running the industry landed the company in trouble. The bankers refused to consider any further loans and asked the unit to bring in additional capital by raising equity through various sources.

While the bank sees the over-expanded capacity as greed, the entrepreneur says he is only ambitious. Apart from improving the management to professional level, thanks to his dealer network and social marketing, the unit has revived.

Case Study 6: PICKLES HECKLE

Varma Agro Products Private Limited

Varma Agro was started as a cottage industry by the wife of the promoter M.K.D. Prasad. Sensing business opportunity, Prasad later left his full-time job with Hindustan Cables Ltd. and joined the business. Due to growth in the business, the company was converted into partnership firm and subsequently into a Pvt. Ltd company with an investment of Rs 68 lakh (Rs 14 lakh equity and Rs 54 lakh debt).

During 1999-2000 flash floods in the twin cities of Hyderabad and Secunderabad, the entire stock in the factory premises was destroyed. Added to this, the negligence of the bank in insuring the stock (the bank usually takes an authorisation from the unit for paying the annual premium by debiting to the unit's account) plunged the company in red. (The losses accumulated to Rs 5.33 lakh)

The unit had good demand both from domestic and foreign markets (US). Most of his former friends heckle him for having got into the pickles business. The promoter was of the opinion that necessary infrastructure in the industrial areas is essential for the smooth functioning of the firm.

Case Study 7: SUN REFUSES TO SHINE ON SUNNY NEEM

Sunny Neem Extracts Pvt. ltd.

Sunny Neem Industries was set up by an IIT-graduate with nearly three decades of experience in supplying equipment to the Railways as a small-scale venture. He and his family members together own about 150 acres of land—about 32 km from Hyderabad where a mango orchard of nearly 30 acres exist. He saw an opportunity in neem as a bio-pesticide applicant in 1995. SIDBI processed a term loan of Rs 92 lakh against the collateral securities of all his land and appurtenances. The value of hypothecated moveables and machinery that extracts neem oil and cake is Rs 1.25 crore. The value of buildings thereon would approximately be Rs 1 crore. The lands being on the approach road to the new international airport of Hyderabad could conservatively be valued at least another Rs 2 crore.

All these securities have been taken as collateral by SIDBI with a second charge by SBI that had granted working capital of Rs 95 lakh in 1995. The market rate for neem oil took a beating in 1998 from Rs 40 to Rs 15 per kg due to liberalisation of tariffs and consequent imports. SIDBI had sanctioned the term loan in September 1995 at 19 per cent p.a. with the condition that the first installment should commence 18 months after the first date of disbursement. Usually a development bank,, that too meant for small industries, should have started recovery of installments 18 months after the completion of the project or the date of final disbursement, whichever is earlier. Thus, the onerous condition of repayment fixation coupled with high interest-rate left no gestation for this industry.

The industry was working capital-intensive as it had to collect neem seeds during a short period of two months and store these combustible neem seeds safely for the rest of the year to allow the factory produce neem oil. SBI had sanctioned working capital at 18.5 per cent p.a. against the second charge of the properties mortgaged to SIDBI. When the market for neem oil and neem cake started eroding in 1998 due to the policy of liberalisation, the unit had to quickly shift to alternate lines of production producing (i) emulsifiable neem oil for pesticide (ii) urea coating agent and (iii) azadirachtin extraction from neem oil for export. It had sought a term loan from SIDBI for additional investment to the tune of Rs 50 lakh. SIDBI took six months to appraise it, during which the entrepreneur chipped in additional investments as he had to use the combustible raw material for alternate production. SIDBI, after sanction of the two term loans, insisted on conversion of the agricultural land where the plant was running in non-agricultural land.

The pleadings of the entrepreneur and the confirmation from the Commissioner of Industries that such conversion was not required for agro-based industry, fell on deaf ears at SIDBI. The entrepreneur, with no option, went around the Ranga Reddy District Administration for two years to get the Conversion Certificate. After he got the Conversion Certificate, SIDBI refused to release the second term loan on the ground that the unit fell in arrears of interest payment and that the term loan itself lapsed and, therefore, required re-appraisal. In the interim, SBI also classified the industry as NPA. Legal proceedings from both lenders led to the collapse of the entrepreneur. The entrepreneur died in penury within the next two years.

18

Strategies Matter for MSME Sector

All the leading commercial banks hesitate to lend to the MSME sector. SMEs on growth path are overawed by the equity markets and latch to the debt markets notwithstanding the travails that they are used to. Most micro and small enterprises lack knowledge in accountancy and negotiating contracts. Negative growth in lending to the sector is worrisome as employment dwindles. Manufacturing clusters are not attracting investors in the MSME sector for want of dependable infrastructure.

Hence attracting investments in the small enterprise sector in Telangana would very much depend upon the improvements in general and project specific infrastructure and effectiveness in implementing the already announced policies like the amendments to the rules under the Factories Act and other Labour Laws, TS-iPass (Telangana State Industrial Project Approval and Self-Certification System) Act 2014, envisaged Sick Industries Revival and Rehabilitation Policy, establishment of Industrial Health Clinic as NBFC with a corpus of Rs 100 crore through private equity participation etc.

There may, sometimes, be a case for governments to protect enterprises in infant stage from unfettered competition. But such protection, not necessarily through tariffs that would protect all domestic enterprises to the same degree, could find ways to help innovators better than imitators. In many fields, the savings that sheer size once made possible are fading as new technologies make customisation cheap, inventories small and capital requirements low.

Telangana state took full advantage of the existing IT infrastructure and innovated into creating a unique model in T-Hub and established RICH (Research and Innovation Circle of Hyderabad) to integrate laboratories to machine production. Its continuing efforts to create manufacturing niche through investments that would anchor micro and small enterprises would take at least another year or two. Linking technical education with skill development would erelong create entrepreneurs and employment on sustainable basis.

One would only wonder then about the reasons for slow progress in Make-in-Telangana. The policy to reach grassroots requires robust institutional interventions. While the reach of the citizens to district administration has improved with the new map of Telangana of 31 districts, in so far as MSMEs are concerned, the District Industries Centres (DICs) are not on the lips of entrepreneurs. Most DICs reaped comfort in releasing subsidies for transport vehicles and little for manufacturing because the latter requires officials' guidance and effort.

Therefore, there is need for renewed policy thrust and specific strategies to rejuvenate the state's manufacturing sector in the MSME space. The chart below outlines a few of them:

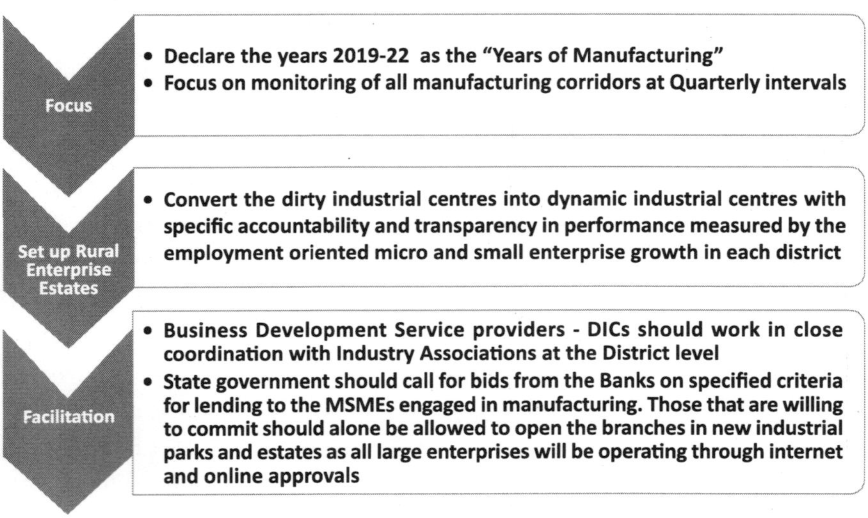

Clean up the Corridor (CUTCOR)

The DICs should survey each Industrial Estate and identify the infrastructure deficiencies. Such survey should be done through CUTCOR Committee consisting of Financing Institution Representatives, Technology Experts, Labour, Energy and Environment experts.

The Survey findings would throw up viability gaps and infrastructure gaps in the various industrial estates. International funding institutions should be approached for sprucing up infrastructure within set time frame on PPP mode.

The CUTCOR Committee will monitor the decisions for effective implementation by all the stakeholders on time-bound schedules.

- This Committee will also screen proposals of allotment of space for new enterprises to come up
- Blacktopping of all main and sub-arteries in the Corridor after estimating the load-carrying capacities of the trucks that pass through the Corridor so that repairs would be minimum
- All wiring would be underground through weather-insulated pipes
- All the corridors are Industrial Zones
- The Lung spaces, Residential areas/complexes, Heavy Transport Parking Bays with full amenities, Environment Protection measures, including air, sound and water treatment measures should be evolved within the next six months – again through Industry Associations' active participation
- A road map with clear milestones should be prepared and implemented by the Empowered Committee
- Each District should have one Rural Enterprise Estate with comprehensive forward and backward linkages, logistics, quality testing and branding facilities in the Sub-Industrial Hubs networked with the Industrial Hub at the state level for market promotion and development
- Allowing eateries/cafeteria only at specific points inside the estate premises with conditions imposed on clean upkeep of the area by these catering units

- Augmentation in supply of water to the units, and provision of drinking water at some fixed, convenient locations

Industrial Technology Network (TECHNO-NET)

Each Industrial Corridor would have to avoid the miscommunication that can arise with adverse consequences for diffusion of more efficient or appropriate technologies for the small industries through networking of technology applications and knowledge bases. The existing knowledge centres, skill development centres, large, medium and small industries should be brought under the fold of TI-Techno-net. The Techno-net should provide guidance and assistance in:

- The preparation of product and engineering designs
- The application of specific process technologies
- Managerial guidance
- Technology information and guidance
- Market information

Techno-net should, in effect, have the network of:

- Education, Research and Development Institutions: Strengthen the existing R&D institutions, universities etc., and reorient their research and management courses to the requirements of the corridors. Industry would be requiring more welders, turners, CAD/CAM operators etc. Existing Technical Education institutions should be fine-tuned for creating new courses and syllabi in an ongoing consultation with the Industry. RICH would widen its scope to cover this aspect
- The state government should ensure industry participation in consultation with Industry Associations in the Board of Studies of the Universities
- Technology-based Training Institutions to frame appropriate syllabi and review it on annual basis three months ahead of the commencement of academic year

- ❖ Testing laboratories should be established in all the Industrial Estates (existing and future) with Industry Associations investing in them under PPP arrangement
- ❖ The supply of basic infrastructure should always exceed the demand at all stages of development
- ❖ Establish a numerically strong and well-equipped security force in the estate

Although it is laudable to entrust the civic administration to the Industrial Area Local Authorities, these bodies cannot clean up the amenities to the levels from where it would be easier for them to maintain. Hence, the state government/TSIIC should bring the level of maintenance in most of the Industrial Estates in the state from where it will be easier for them to take off.

Annual Returns on Production by units shall all be submitted online. There is already a provision to this effect in the state although monitoring mechanisms fall short. After providing an initial corpus fund required for carrying out these tasks, the state government can pay for services and network costs. Small action groups can be formed for the purpose.

Model PPP agreements for the MSME sector should take into account the disabilities of the sector and should necessarily provide for arbitration clause so that recourse to legal action by the involved parties shall be the minimum and as last resort.

The governments and PSUs shall under all circumstances resolve the conflicts in payments and services only through arbitration within the framework of the Arbitration Act and MSME Development Act.

ANNEXURE

Policies of the State Governments

State governments have the primary responsibility for the development of MSMEs. Each state, depending upon its own endowment and strengths, has carved out a policy for the sector that largely defines the infrastructure and incentive boundaries related to all the factors of production—land, labour, capital and organisation. Most states have a shared vision of creating a vibrant MSME sector with a view to competing for spreading the red carpet to the investors. Cooperative Federalism also requires effective coordination and cooperation between the Union and the states, particularly in regard to subjects that are on the Concurrent List of the Constitution of India.

In this section we deal with a few states that have made difference from others and improved ease of doing business for the MSMEs. The state policies that deserve a close look are: Andhra Pradesh, Chhattisgarh, Gujarat, Haryana, Punjab, Karnataka, Kerala, Madhya Pradesh, Rajasthan, Tamil Nadu and Telangana. These 11 states have 72 per cent of MSME investments in the country according to the 4th Census of SSIs. However, we are documenting a brief of AP, Gujarat, Chhattisgarh, Madhya Pradesh, Kerala and Telangana that have demonstrated success in ease of doing business for MSMEs.

Andhra Pradesh

The Andhra Pradesh Industrial Development Policy, 2015-20 aims to establish state-of-the-art infrastructure, promote manufacturing, enhance inclusivity, foster innovation and create employment opportunities across sectors. The state intends to be the most preferred destination for investors by providing favourable business climate, excellent infrastructure, good law and order and peaceful industrial relations. The new industrial policy focuses on creating a conducive eco-system which makes industries based in Andhra Pradesh innovative and globally competitive.

Vision: "To make Andhra Pradesh a progressive and highly industrialised state... a state that is a centre of technology and innovation... And, a joyous population confident of its bright future..."

The state's policy objectives include ensuring sustainable and inclusive industrial growth to be among the top three states in the country in terms of industrial investments by 2022. It had set its sights high to be the most preferred logistics hub and India's gateway to East and Southeast Asia by 2029 through quantitative and qualitative skilled manpower. It also aims to create significant employment opportunities.

Instruments are: Single Desk Clearance with e-platform facilitating all necessary clearances for starting and operating an industry within 21 working days through online filing and tracking of pre-operation stage clearances. Spot approvals deemed approvals on self-certification basis, assignment of inspection to competent private technical experts are other integral parts of the policy.

Chhattisgarh

While this state had also formulated like the other progressive states its policy objectives on the same lines, for purposes of industrial promotion, it had classified industries into saturated, priority sector, core sector and general category.

Its interest subsidy scheme is different from the other states while the capital subsidy scheme for MSEs had a ceiling of Rs 60 lakh for priority category and Rs 30 lakh for general category with a ceiling of

30 per cent of the total investment. Medium enterprises and SC/ST entrepreneurs have different levels of incentive systems. The policy for incentives thus is on equity considerations keeping in view the need for high level of growth of industrial sector.

Interest subsidy that is provided to the MSEs on risk optimisation model is worthy of emulation by the other states.

Gujarat

"The Gujarat Industrial Policy 2015 is more a framework than a detailed blueprint."

Vision: By making Gujarat as an attractive "Total Business Destination", expedite the overall country's economic growth, thereby increasing the standard of living and prosperity among the people of Gujarat by giving them the opportunity for skilled employment and nurtured enterprises. Main objectives of the policy:

- To create employment opportunities for both skilled and unskilled workforce;
- To become a global hub for manufacturing;
- To promote Ease of Doing Business to create business friendly environment;
- To provide pro-active support to micro, small and medium enterprises;
- To promote the spirit of innovation and incentivise entrepreneurship among youth by providing specific sector skills and seed capital.

This support will come by way of interest subsidy for manufacturing and service sector, venture capital assistance, quality certification, technology acquisition fund, patent assistance for national and international, energy and water conservation audit, market development assistance and support, MSMEs for credit rating, raising capital through SME exchange, reimbursement of CGTSME scheme for collateral free loan, state awards under MSMEs and skill development etc.

Technology support

The Upgradation of the existing technology is a requirement of modern industrialisation process to ensure supreme quality. The policy intends to build a technology acquisition fund to be able to extend financial assistance to industrial enterprises intending to upgrade their technological setup.

Financial support will be provided to each cluster for every innovative technology they adopt and introduce in the manufacturing process

Market Development initiatives

The Gujarat government is taking adequate steps with the intention of giving enhanced visibility to local produce from large industries and specifically from MSMEs. Cognizant of the efforts required to make global distribution of local products a reality, in accordance with the national 'Make In India' policy, the Government of Gujarat stresses on 'Zero Defect' to produce globally-competitive, locally manufactured goods. It

Gujarat thus has provided enhanced support systems for technology upgradation and marketing that we do not see in other states.

Kerala

The state's physical quality of life, high level of out-migration, high share of foreign remittances in the state income implies a peculiar pattern of development and policies. It is one of the high wage islands in the country. Even amidst crisis and political sensitivities, the state attained a growth rate of 9.51 per cent in 2014 compared to the national average of 6.2 per cent. The MSME sector is heavily weighted towards the micro enterprises and, therefore, the policies of this state become important. (ISED MSME Development Report 2014, p.161)

Industrial and Commercial Policy 2011 laid special emphasis on MSMEs. The major objective of the policy is development of more enterprises by fortifying the skilled human capital and promoting investments, including domestic as well as foreign, in all the sectors.

While laying emphasis on industrial infrastructure and cluster development, it laid emphasis on the following:

An MSME Equity participation fund for encouraging startups will be created in the Kerala State Industrial Development Corporation and Kerala Financial Corporation.

- Exemption for payment of EMD and security deposit and price preference to MSME may be continued for a period of 5 years. Purchase preference for SMEs in the state for PSUs/LSG procurement will be institutionalised.
- Industrial Adalats will be organised regularly at district/state level with a view to understanding the problems of MSMEs and to settle pending issues.
- Skilled workers to industrial units will be facilitated through Employability centres under the Labour and Skills department.
- To encourage women to take up entrepreneurship as a career the industries set up by them will be treated under the thrust industry category enabling them to avail 30 per cent investment subsidy.

Madhya Pradesh

- The state's policy provides for level playing field for all investors, a single window system – MPTRIFAC, fiscal and financial incentives, concessions and exemptions, supportive land allocation for industrial projects, upgradation of industrial infrastructure, promotion of ancillary units to promote local vendors, enhancing employability of youth through skill development efforts, ensuring harmony between private investors and local citizens through Dispute Resolution mechanism, specific sector promotion policies establishing a broadband, and promoting industrial parks for new clusters of MSEs in different parts of the state.
- Eighteen services automated for delivery through the single window system.
- District Trade and Industry Centres strengthened by modern technology and capacity building of staff. District level

committees are empowered to decide on issues of sanction and disbursal of incentives under approved policies.

- ❖ The Pollution Control Board had to review the certification once in every 3 years for all the categories that have been issued PCB clearances. It had introduced capital subsidy for green industrialisation. It had established a Corpus Fund of Rs 100 crore in September 2016 to provide equity support for the MSMEs.

Telangana

Telangana, the 29th and newest state of India, has formulated a dynamic industrial policy acclaimed as the best in the country distancing itself from several legacy issues. Its Vision: Research to Innovation, Innovation to Industry and Industry to Prosperity". Its core values are:

- ❖ Regulatory framework shall facilitate industrial growth
- ❖ Industrialisation shall be inclusive and facilitate social equality
- ❖ Entrepreneurs will thrive in a peaceful, secure and progressive business regulatory environment
- ❖ Industrial development should lead to massive job creation benefitting local youth
- ❖ Environment shall be protected.

It has mandated minimum inspection and maximum facilitation.

Instruments

While several states claimed Single Window introduction for granting clearances, TSiPASS of Government of Telangana stood the test of Ease of Doing Business with its innate strengths relating to: 1. Online clearances in one go; 2. Tracking and tracing the application; 3. Specific timelines in responsiveness of various departments; 4. Deemed approvals and 5. Penalties on the delays. Similarly, land and labour issues resolved by the Government of Telangana also received commendation. For example, regarding inspections, Inspections cannot be done at will. Due notice must be given to the Enterprises for inspections and Inspection Reports have to be shared with the enterprises for rectifications, if any.

MSMEs are encouraged to access skill building initiatives of the state government like the T-Hub and TASK: (Telangana Academy of Skills and Knowledge), Research & Innovation Circle of Hyderabad (RICH), Telangana Industrial Health Clinic Ltd., for revival of micro and small manufacturing enterprises, a unique co-financing and Fintech (TIHCL) etc., set up under PPP model. Model of Telangana has come up for replication across the country for institutional innovations.

Among the BDS providers, TANSTIA and CODISSIA of Tamil Nadu, KASSIA of Karnataka, FISME, India SME Forum of New Delhi at the national level were cited for best practices.

TS-PRIDE (Telangana State Programme for Rapid Incubation for Dalit Entrepreneurs) for Dalit entrepreneurs has been put in place. SC/ST Hubs and WeHub have been established with a view to enhancing the reach of the schemes meant for these vulnerable sections speedily. All the DICs have been mandated to hold awareness workshops and ensure active post-workshop engagement to ensure enterprise creation.

RICH (Research and Innovation Circle of Hyderabad) – Recognizing the gap in the innovation-entrepreneurship-investment ecosystem, the state intends to create a platform in the RICH linking a host of research institutions, academia and industry through an SPV and a Research to Market Fund (RMF) to fund entrepreneurship activity is proposed in the Policy.

The government set up Industrial Health Clinic (a FINTECH NBFC) as an independent autonomous entity with an initial stakeholder-participated corpus fund of Rs.100 crore.

Briefly put, the objectives of setting up the IHC Corpus Fund are:

- ❖ Promoting a Comprehensive Financial Service Team with Accredited Consultants providing diagnostic assistance;
- ❖ Consulting services in finance, marketing, branding, co-branding, technology through a team of accredited consultants with pre-decided tariffs with transparence and accountability;

- ❖ Help manufacturing start-ups & Incubation Centres;
- ❖ Help preparation of operating plans prior to submission to the FIs/Banks;
- ❖ Expand the financing channel available to MSEs to resolve issues relating to working capital;
- ❖ Help conducting Techno-economic Valuation studies when the viability of the functioning of MSE faces the threat;
- ❖ Help the MSEs in revival and rehabilitation through effective guidance and timely supplementation of financial resources; and
- ❖ Identify the strategic partnership firms for creating a comfort zone to the banks to revive the MSEs so that the units come out of the NPA status.

It is but a surprise that with such progressive policies enveloping the states and Union, MSMEs should continue to be a depressed lot warranting special attention time and again.

Policy delivery needs to be cleaned up and this would mean cleaning up old institutions and setting up new institutions where necessary with specific focus. Second, one important aspect we noticed is that most of the states did not provide budget outlays consistent with the plethora of announced policy incentives and even where the budgets are announced they were not released in time. A holistic view needs to be taken to ensure that the policy instruments and delivery systems should be in sync with intent and there should be a regulatory review annually for taking midcourse corrections. It is this backdrop that made the present government take a holistic view of MSME sector.

Guiding Factors for the Future Policy Direction

Policy Formulation is bounded by political feasibility, economic efficiency, and acceptability to a broad coalition between different players. Cooperative Federalism will broadly guide the destiny of future.

The Drivers:

1. Expanding ecosystem for easy start-up and *market exit*
    - Expanding the basis for growth of start-up enterprises

- Reforming start-up related regulations and procedure
- Conducting business conversion and restructuring

2. *Fostering creative innovation ability*

- Developing new technology and facilitating commercialisation
- Fostering market-friendly venture business environment
- Strengthening capacity for management innovation

3. *Expanding basis for competition and growth*

- Providing policy finance based on future value
- Thorough overhaul of the financial regulations and institutions with specific orientation to MSEs
- Rural Enterprise Promotion with focus on preventing out-migration and promote local employment and local skills and local resources
- Expanding consumer market and promoting exports
- Upgrading manpower structure and improving demand and supply

4. *Alleviating polarisation through mutual growth*

- Strengthening practical cooperation between large and small business
- Enhanced Role for the Business Development Services
- Ensuring competitive micro-enterprises
- Assisting local, women-owned, handicapped-run Business Practical Service for SMEs
- Comprehensive counseling system; Quality control of zero-defect policy.

These progressive policies are the *raison d'etre* for the state realising 70 per cent of promised investments in large, small and medium enterprises space.

Index